Quiet Riots

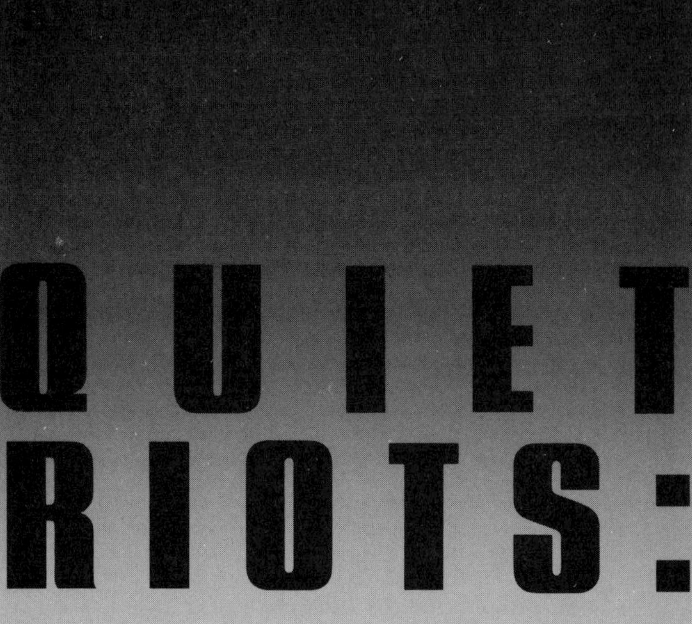

Race and Poverty in the United States

Edited by Fred R. Harris and Roger W. Wilkins

The Kerner Report Twenty Years Later

Pantheon Books  New York

 Published in the United States by Pantheon Books, a division of Random House, Inc., New York, and simultaneously in Canada by Random House of Canada Limited, Toronto.

LIBRARY OF CONGRESS CATALOGING-IN-PUBLICATION DATA

Quiet riots.

Includes index.
Contents: The 1967 riots and the Kerner Commission / Fred R. Harris—The Kerner Report / John Herbers—Poverty is still with us—and worse / David Hamilton—[etc.]
1. Urban poor—United States. 2. Afro-Americans—Economic conditions. 3. United States—Race relations. 4. United States—Economic conditions. 5. United States. Kerner Commission. I. Harris, Fred R., 1930- II. Wilkins, Roger W., 1932–
HV4045.Q54 1988 305.5'69'0973 88–42770
ISBN 0–394–57473–7
ISBN 0–679–72100–2 (pbk.)

Manufactured in the United States of America

First Edition

CONTENTS

Part III A Growing Urban Underclass

Part IV Conclusions and Recommendations

ACKNOWLEDGMENTS

The editors are grateful to the Johnson Foundation—and especially to William B. Boyd, President; Henry Halstead, Vice-President; Richard Kinch, Program Associate; Susan Poulsen Krogh, Director of Public Information and Program Extension; and Kay Mauer, Conference Coordinator—for co-sponsoring and expertly assisting with the February 1988 conference, The Kerner Report: Twenty Years Later, held at the foundation's Wingspread Conference Center in Racine, Wisconsin, out of which this book grew. Warm appreciation is also expressed to the University of New Mexico Institute for Public Policy, the principal sponsor of the conference, and to Margaret S. Elliston, Research Associate with the institute, Paul L. Hain, Chair of the UNM Political Science Department, and Al Stotts of UNM Public Affairs for their help. Special thanks, too, to David Sternbach, editor at Pantheon Books, for his encouragement and valuable assistance in the preparation of this book.

INTRODUCTION

"Our nation is moving toward two societies, one black, one white—separate and unequal."

Those blunt words were published twenty years ago by the Kerner Commission (the President's National Advisory Commission on Civil Disorders).

President Lyndon B. Johnson appointed the Kerner Commission in the summer of 1967. Riots had devastated the black sections of many of America's major cities. Detroit was burning, and U.S. Army troops had been sent there to quell the disorders. Central Newark was in ruins.

The Kerner Report—dated March 1, 1968—looked beyond the riots, as members of the commission immediately found they had to do, to racism and poverty and the other terrible, underlying conditions out of which the riots had mushroomed. The report called for great new efforts to combat American poverty, unemployment, and racism. It gave America a much more accurate picture of where we were and where we might be heading than anyone could reasonably have expected from what many had thought to be a pretty middle-of-the-road group of commissioners. The report was a measure of America's failure of vision up to then—and, sadly, it is a measure of our failure of will in recent years.

Twenty years ago, both Dr. Martin Luther King, Jr., and Robert F. Kennedy had almost a year left to live. Despite the riots, there was a high and hopeful energy in ghettos all over the country. The Civil Rights Act was three years old, and the Voting Rights Act and the War on Poverty were even younger. For years, America had enjoyed a rising gross national product and both low inflation and low unemployment rates. The economic and social costs of the Vietnam War had not yet debilitated the country. The rising tide of black consciousness and the experiments with maximum feasible participation of the poor (community-action programs), together with the momentary idealism of the leaders of many urban-centered corporations, gave glimpses of a better day around the corner.

And, for a good many black people, a better day did come. There are black mayors now, in Newark and Detroit and a number of other cities, including, of all places, Birmingham. There are black millionaires in Los Angeles, New York, and in a number of towns in between. Blacks have jobs none would have dreamed of fifty years ago.

But neither economic progress for some blacks nor increased black political power have made a significant difference for the poor blacks left behind—nor for other minorities and poor people generally. For those who are still poor today—and there are more of them now, minority and nonminority, urban as well as rural—life is even harder, meaner than it was twenty years ago. For them, there is more despair now, less hope, and less chance of escape.

But most Americans probably do not know that, and

assume that the progress we made for a time after the Kerner Report has continued up to the present. It has not.

So, on the eve of the twentieth anniversary of the Kerner Report, we set up a nongovernmental 1988 Commission on the Cities to assess our present situation in terms of race, poverty, and unemployment—and to make new recommendations about what should be done.

The 1988 Commission on the Cities, together with the University of New Mexico Institute for Public Policy and the Johnson Foundation, brought together a distinguished group of experts in a national conference: The Kerner Report: Twenty Years Later. The two of us cochaired the commission and the conference. Other participants included William R. Carmack, University of Oklahoma; Jorge Chapa, University of California at Berkeley; Lynn A. Curtis, Milton S. Eisenhower Foundation; Greg J. Duncan, University of Michigan; Margaret S. Elliston, University of New Mexico; David Ginsburg, attorney, Washington, D.C.; David Hamilton, University of New Mexico; LaDonna Harris, Americans for Indian Opportunity; John Herbers, University of Maryland; Ronald B. Mincy, University of Delaware and the Urban Institute; Gary Orfield, University of Chicago; Gary D. Sandefur, University of Wisconsin at Madison; Gregory D. Squires, University of Wisconsin at Milwaukee; Al Stotts, University of New Mexico; Henry B. Taliaferro, Jr., attorney, Oklahoma City; F. Harold Wilson, Bowdoin College; and William Julius Wilson, University of Chicago. Also participating in the conference, but not present when the report of the 1988 commission was adopted, were Richard P. Nathan, Princeton University, and Donna E. Shalala, chancellor of the University of Wisconsin at Madison.

This book is a product of that conference. The full report of the 1988 Commission on the Cities is printed as the final chapter of this volume, Chapter 9. A summary of the report was also adopted, and will serve well as an introduction to what the contributors to this book have to say about race and poverty in the United States twenty years after the Kerner Report:

For a time after the Kerner Report, and through the mid-1970s, we made progress on all fronts. Then came a series of economic shocks: recessions, manufacturing moves and closings, the flight of jobs and the middle class to the suburbs, and a reduction in real wages. These blows hit the most vulnerable Americans hardest. There were determined efforts to cut social programs in education, housing, jobs, training, and other areas. The Reagan administration was hostile to affirmative action and to vigorous enforcement of the civil-rights laws.

What is the present situation on race and poverty in the United States?

- **Poverty is worse now than it was twenty years ago. More people are poor—both white and nonwhite. Those who are poor are poorer. Escape from poverty is harder. Overall unemployment in America is twice what it was twenty years ago. And unemployment for blacks is now twice what it is for whites.**

- **The Kerner Report is coming true: America *is* again becoming two societies, one black (and, today, we can add to that, Hispanic), one white—separate and unequal.**

- **There is a large and growing urban underclass in America—principally made up of blacks and Hispanics in the central cities. They are more economically isolated, more socially alienated, than ever before.**

There are "quiet riots" in all of America's central cities: unemployment, poverty, social disorganization, segregation, family disintegration, housing and school deterioration, and crime are worse now. These "quiet riots" are not as alarming as the violent riots of twenty years ago, or as noticeable to outsiders. But they are even more destructive of human life. National security requires renewed human investment if we are to be a stable and secure society of self-esteem. We have the means. We must summon the will.

FRED R. HARRIS
ROGER W. WILKINS

Quiet Riots

Part I

THE KERNER REPORT OF 1968

"The only genuine, long-range solution for what has happened lies in an attack—mounted at every level—upon the conditions that breed despair and violence," President Lyndon Johnson said in a nationwide address on July 27, 1967, when he announced the appointment of the President's National Advisory Commission on Civil Disorders—the Kerner Commission.

"All of us know what those conditions are: ignorance, discrimination, slums, poverty, disease, not enough jobs," the president continued. "We should attack these conditions—not because we are frightened by conflict, but because we are fired by conscience. We should attack them because there is simply no other way to achieve a decent and orderly society in America."

President Johnson was right, though he was still to be distressed by the commission's eventual findings and recommendations, which turned out to be almost exactly in line with his own words when he created the commission.

Here, in Chapters 1 and 2, we have the accounts of two eyewitnesses, so to speak, to the Kerner Commission's work. Fred R. Harris, the author of Chapter 1, was a U.S. Senator at the time and a member of the Kerner Commission. John Herbers, author of Chapter 2, covered the commission for the *New York Times.* Though they differ somewhat on present recommendations, Herbers declaring more faith in the efforts of the states and private business, and Harris calling for renewed federal action, they provide dramatic pictures of the conditions that led to the appointment of the Kerner Commission, as well as special insights on its report and what happened, or did not happen, as a result.

CHAPTER 1

The 1967 Riots and the Kerner Commission

FRED R. HARRIS

NOBODY REALIZED, WHEN Watts blew up in the summer of 1965, that it was a portent of things to come in many of America's cities.

A routine traffic arrest sparked the riot in Watts, a black section of Los Angeles. A white police officer stopped a twenty-one-year-old black man two blocks from his home. The man's mother and brother intervened. It was a hot August evening, and that small incident was all it took to ignite the frustrations, hostilities, and tensions that had been building up for years in Watts. A crowd gathered, and an ugly mood grew and erupted into violence.

For some time, blacks, mostly poor and from the South

and looking for work, had been streaming into Los Angeles County at the rate of 30,000 a year. Their numbers had swollen to 650,000 by 1965, too many of them packed into the insufficient housing of Watts. Two-thirds of black high-school students in Watts were dropping out of their over-crowded and inferior schools before graduation. Two-thirds of the adults lacked high-school diplomas. Black unemployment in the county was about three times that for whites—forty percent of Watts residents had no automobiles, and there was no public transportation to take them to the jobs in the suburbs.[1]

Thirty-four people were killed in the Watts riot, which, before it was quelled, had spread over forty-six square miles. Over a thousand people were injured, four thousand were arrested, and property damage was estimated at $40 million. A riot commission appointed by California's governor issued a report ominously titled: *Violence in the City—an End or a Beginning?*

Ghetto riots had erupted in Harlem the preceding year and in Chicago that very summer. In fact, there had been black protests, uprisings, disorders, and violence ever since black people were first brought to this continent as slaves. Black-white tensions had always been especially heightened during wartime and immediately afterwards. Blacks were drafted like everyone else to fight in America's wars, of course, and, when black veterans let it be known afterward that they expected better treatment at home, they often brought down on their heads a terrible and violent white backlash.

This was true, for example, with World War I, in which 350,000 American blacks served, 42,000 of them in combat. In 1917, thirty-nine blacks and nine whites were killed and hundreds were injured when whites rioted in East St. Louis and destroyed three hundred buildings in the black section there. The same year, there were "race riots" in Philadelphia and Chester, Pennsylvania. There were thirty deaths and hundreds of injuries in a race riot in Chicago in 1919, a year in which there were similar disorders in Omaha, Nashville, Charleston, and Washington, D.C. A white mob in Tulsa destroyed a square mile of the black section of that city in a horrible 1921 race riot that killed over thirty people.

Again, during and after World War II, there were urban disorders and violent racial clashes in Mobile, Los Angeles, Beaumont, Harlem, St. Louis, Youngstown, Cicero, and Chicago. Federal troops were called out to quell a 1943 riot in Detroit that resulted in the deaths of twenty-five blacks and nine whites, injuries to hundreds, and the destruction of over $200 million worth of property.

Beginning after World War II, there was a massive and accelerating influx of blacks into America's cities, as they sought to escape the wretched poverty and brutal degradation of the rural and small-town South. They moved to places like Detroit and Newark on word-of-mouth rumors of jobs that too often proved to be mere vapors. Racial segregation was as rigid in the North as what they had known in the South. Three and four families rented rooms in old single-family houses in what were now all-black sections of the central cities. The housing projects were packed. And still the blacks came, looking for work—just when many of the better manufacturing jobs were beginning to disappear altogether or were being moved to the white suburbs.

Black frustrations rose, but so did black expectations—especially as a result of civil-rights activism and laws and the antipoverty and other programs of the 1960s. Clearly, the combination was explosive. As de Tocqueville wrote, "Evils which are patiently endured when they seem inevitable become intolerable when once the idea of escape from them is suggested."

Consider Newark in 1967. Between 1960 and 1966, Newark had changed from 65 percent white to 62 percent nonwhite, as blacks moved in and whites moved out. Still, there were only two black members on Newark's seven-member city council, and the white mayor, over black objections, had just appointed a white secretary of the school board. Central-city housing was rundown and deteriorating, neighborhoods dismal. The official black unemployment rate was 12 percent. Forty percent of black children lived in single-parent homes. Newark's schools, where student enrollment had grown by a third since the late 1950s and where much less was spent per child than in the white suburbs, had a dropout rate of 33 percent; about half of all blacks from sixteen to nineteen years old were not in school. The city had the highest crime rate in the country.

The situation in Detroit was no better. Its black population had grown by 40 percent in the six years prior to 1967. Detroit schools, up 60,000 in enrollments during that same period, were 57 percent black and would have required seventeen hundred more teachers and a thousand more classrooms just to come up to average state standards. The dropout rate in Detroit schools was 50 percent. Surrounding suburban schools were annually spending $500 more per student. In Detroit's black Twelfth Street area, where 21,000 people were crowded into each square mile (twice Detroit's average), more than a fourth of the apartment buildings were so rundown as to require demolition, and another 20 percent were below livable standards.

During the summer of 1966, a year after the prophetic Watts riot, urban disorders occurred in twenty communities—the largest in Chicago, San Francisco, and the Hough section of Cleveland. But these disorders were small indeed compared to the terrible explosions that came during the next, "long hot summer" of 1967—the worst being in Newark and Detroit.

Just as in Watts, seemingly random sparks ignited black frustrations in Newark. The all-white police force, as all around America, became the focus of black hostilities toward an unresponsive system. Indeed, the police were about the only part of the system with which many blacks had any contact at all.

On a hot July night in 1967, a Newark police car stopped a taxi driven by a black man whose license had been revoked. The man, one John Smith, was taken to the Fourth Precinct station, where a number of blacks watched out front as he was dragged and carried, unable or unwilling to walk, from the police car and into the precinct house. Reports and rumors spread. A hostile crowd gathered. Police reinforcements arrived. Tensions increased. Two black mediators tried unsuccessfully to calm and disperse the crowd. Suddenly, a Molotov cocktail crashed against the station wall. The police scattered the crowd, and quiet returned for a time.

Not for long. The next day, the mayor agreed to an investigation of Smith's arrest and treatment, declaring it "an isolated incident." A black "Police Brutality Rally" in front of the precinct station got out of hand after the rumor spread that Smith had died. Young blacks began roaming the streets, breaking windows. This disorder grew rapidly. Looting, burning, and damage to property mounted. There were reports of gunshots.

Local law-enforcement officials were soon joined by state police and the New Jersey National Guard. Untrained and not knowing what to do, these often-frightened young men frequently fired their weapons indiscriminately. Before it was all over, twenty-five people were dead in Newark, twenty-one of them innocent civilians (including, for example, the eleven-year-old black youngster who carried out the garbage from his apartment and died from a gunshot as his mother watched from a window, and a black woman who died at her project window, killed by National Guard fire). Six of the civilian dead were women. Several were children. Damage to property was estimated at $10.2 million, primarily in lost merchandise. Damage to buildings and fixtures alone was estimated at $2 million.

A little over a week later, Detroit's time was up. The police raided a "blind pig," an illegal after-hours drinking joint at the corner of Twelfth Street and Clairmont. They had expected to find ten to twenty people. Instead, they arrested eighty-two and herded them down to the street to wait for more patrol wagons. A crowd of about two hundred blacks gathered very rapidly, and their initial good humor quickly changed to surliness. A bottle was thrown against a police-car window. The riot began. False rumors spread about the arresting methods used by the police officers. By the next morning, the crowd numbered into the thousands. Looting, window-breaking, and burning were widespread. The state police were called in, then the National Guard—and finally, on President Johnson's orders, federal troops.

Thirty-three blacks and ten whites were killed in the Detroit riot; seventeen of these were looters (including two white men). Two of the deaths resulted from a fallen power line. Seventeen of the dead were killed by accidental gunshots or were murdered. Two persons were burned to death. One police officer was killed accidentally by another officer while he was scuffling with a looter. One white man was killed by a rioter. The injured numbered 279, including 85 police officers. Damage estimates ranged up to $45 million. Nearly 700 buildings were burned, 412 of them being totally destroyed. Over seven thousand people were arrested.

Sadly—and alarmingly—there was more. There were major riots that summer, too, in Atlanta, Buffalo, Cambridge, Maryland, Cincinnati, Grand Rapids, Milwaukee, Minneapolis, Tampa, and Plainfield, New Jersey. Twenty-eight other cities had serious disorders, lasting one to two days, and ninety-two cities had smaller outbreaks. In all, this violence brought death to eighty-four people, injuries to several hundred more, and property damage of between $75 and $100 million.

I was a member of the U.S. Senate from Oklahoma at that time. In this crisis atmosphere, I went to the Senate floor and proposed that the president appoint a blue-ribbon commission to look into the causes and prevention of urban violence, declaring "that lawlessness and violence cannot be tolerated in a society which is based upon law, that law and order must be accompanied by justice, and that equality of social, economic, and political opportunity must be made real, immediately, for all Americans."

After telephoning me at home to say that he was going to make me a member of it, Lyndon Johnson went on television to announce the creation of the President's National Advisory Commission on Civil Disorders, naming a federal district judge and former Illinois governor, Otto Kerner, to chair it. The commission also included a big-city mayor, John Lindsay of New York; two blacks, U.S. Senator Edward Brooke (R., Mass.) and NAACP head Roy Wilkins; one woman, Kentucky Commerce Secretary Katherine Peden; two House members, James Corman (D., Cal.) and William McCulloch (R., Ohio); a big-city police chief, Herbert Jenkins of Atlanta; a businessman, Charles Thornton of Litton

Industries; and a labor leader, I. W. Abel, head of the Steelworkers. An extremely competent and sensitive Washington attorney, David Ginsburg, was appointed executive director of the commission.

A first-rate staff and an excellent corps of consultants were hired. The commission set to work—on numerous and lengthy hearings and field trips and serious studies.

In his charge to the commission, President Johnson had asked us to answer three basic questions about the riots: "What happened? Why did it happen? What can be done to prevent it from happening again and again?" President Johnson, like a lot of people at the time, thought that there had been some kind of conspiracy behind the disorders; he told me so himself. The commission soon knew that that was not true, that hostility levels were so high in all of America's cities that almost anything could have set them off—and we said so in our report.

At first, we had thought that we should make two reports: a quick one, before the next summer's "riot season" began, that would deal only with short-range solutions for preventing and quelling riots; and a later, deeper, final report that would deal with long-range solutions to the underlying social and economic problems. We soon realized that there were no short-range solutions—the causes of the riots were too deep and serious for that; they grew out of racism and economic deprivation. We determined to make only one report, as soon as we could, and to tell the complete truth about both causes and solutions—the latter to call for great new federal efforts for jobs, training, education, housing, and vigorous civil-rights enforcement.

We knew that our findings and recommendations would be controversial, and we knew that solutions would not be inexpensive. We knew that we had to deal with all kinds of poverty in our report—both minority and nonminority, both urban and rural—because we found, of course, that poverty affected people indiscriminately, whoever they were and wherever they lived, and because there was no legal or political way to offer assistance to some and not to others.

Someone mistakenly told President Johnson that our report would not have a good word to say about his antipoverty and civil-rights efforts, that the report would, in effect, condone—and maybe even encourage—rioting. This was utterly untrue, but President Johnson apparently believed it, as did others. He canceled plans to receive the report in a White House ceremony. He refused to consider the commission's proposal for staying in operation for an additional six months in order to lobby for our recommendations. Somebody bootlegged the report to the *Washington Post,* and, when the newspaper refused to hold up its publication until we could give carefully planned, advance briefings for reporters, we had to dump the report on all the press at once. It was a reporter's nightmare, a madhouse. For example, a writer for the Associated Press called me frantically, with only a thirty-minute deadline after he had received the report, to beg me to "capsulize" its voluminous findings and recommendations.

Despite all this, the report had significant impact. Some years of continued and gradual progress followed. But the Vietnam War and its aftermath, brutal tight-money recessions, accelerated plant closings and displacements, and middle-class flight, were followed by a later antigovernment movement highlighted by cuts in jobs, education, training, and other social programs and by greatly reduced enforcement efforts. All these checked and turned back the progress America had made. What we tried worked, for the most part. We just did not try hard enough. Or we quit trying.

Now, twenty or more years later, things are worse in

places like Watts, Newark, and Detroit. In Watts, for example, unemployment is still much higher than in the rest of Los Angeles, housing projects are rotting, more than half the high-school students drop out before graduation, and fewer of them are going on to college—and as if all that were not enough, there are the terribly increased pestilences of drugs and gangs, too.[2] It is the same story in Newark and Detroit. Detroit is smaller, blacker, and poorer, now. It has lost population as people have moved to the suburbs (down from 1.5 million in 1970 to 1 million today). It has gone from 44 percent black to 66 percent black. At the time of the riots, black unemployment in Detroit was 10 percent; now, nearly one in three blacks in the labor pool is out of work, a 30.7 percent unemployment rate, compared to 13.3 percent for whites.[3]

If things are worse, why aren't blacks rioting today? The Kerner Commission decided that there was no way to say why violence occurred one time and not another, why in one place and not another—why, for example, in Watts in 1965, but not in 1967, why not in Washington, D.C., in 1967, but, later, after Dr. King was assassinated in 1968?

Nobody knows, except that hopeless and despairing people are less likely to cause trouble. There is less hope in the central cities now than there was twenty years ago.

A little over twenty years ago, I remember walking the unswept streets of a black slum of deteriorating houses with fellow Kerner commissioner John Lindsay, and coming upon a group of untrained, poorly educated young black men, idling there, unable to find jobs. At first, they thought we were the "law."

"Who is it, the FBI?" one young man asked. When they found out that we weren't, they all began to talk at once: "We want a job, man. Get us a job. Can't you get us a job? Get us a job. We want a job."

When the chorus died down, one said, "I want a job, man. I've got five kids, and I need a job. Mr. Johnson [President Johnson] got me a job this summer, but it ran out yesterday."

Did they ever find work? Was it steady? I hope so, but I'm doubtful. I know that there are thousands more like them on the streets, now. And I know, too, that that is not good for America. We must renew our commitment to "make good the promises," as the Kerner Report admonished us to do, or face a future of greater poverty and increased instability.

CHAPTER 2

The Kerner Report: A Journalist's View

JOHN HERBERS

THE BEST WAY for me to describe the impact of the Kerner Report is through my own experiences of covering various aspects of race relations, urban affairs, and social and economic trends in the United States over a period that spans almost four decades. I arrived in Washington in 1965, just as the urban riots were beginning, after covering the civil-rights movement in the South. Enactment of the Voting Rights Act that year ended massive white resistance in the South to desegregation and coincided with the splintering of the civil-rights movement between those who wanted to continue Martin Luther King's tactics of nonviolence and integration and those who favored a much more militant approach that was widely interpreted, at least by whites, as moving toward violent protest and self-imposed black separatism.

The two previous decades had seen a revolution that was both remarkable and unique in American history—a series of massive demonstrations and the refusal by blacks to abide by segregation and racially discriminatory laws. This direct action resulted in the national government and its courts invalidating laws and practices that had been entrenched in the South since shortly after the abolition of slavery. Now, in 1965, attention was shifting to northern, western, and also southern cities, where millions of blacks who had fled southern farms and plantations for generations past were locked in urban ghettos where they experienced institutionalized poverty and unemployment. Their plight was no less real than that of poor blacks in the South, and in some ways it was worse. The difference was that there was now no great body of discriminatory law to attack, but a more subtle kind of discrimination that many whites denied existed.

In those days, a buzzword among journalists was that when a president did not know what to do to change a troubling and chronic situation, he would appoint a study commission to recommend what steps he should take, thus avoiding responsibility—at least for the time being. But when he did appoint a commission of highly placed Establishment leaders, the newspapers, particularly those such as the *New York Times,* took the action seriously and gave front-page attention to both the study process and the commission's conclusions. As the reporter most responsible for following urban and racial trends in the United States, I wrote the lead stories for the *Times* on the Kerner Commission's work.

It is hard to overstate the importance that was placed on the commission's report. There were several reasons for this. One was that urban riots of the 1960s were widely considered a major threat to domestic stability. Although race riots had been common in American history, never had there been so many disturbances occurring simultaneously in cities from coast to coast. Many public officials believed that these disorders were either the result of a conspiracy by some persons or organizations to disrupt the society, or the manifestation of an anger on the part of urban blacks that few had detected. There was, therefore, an urgency about detecting the cause, and public interest mounted when the membership of the Kerner Commission turned out to be, for the most part, a cross-section of highly responsible government and business leaders, who themselves assembled a remarkably competent staff of public servants, scholars, and lawyers.

Another reason for the commission's perceived importance was the widely held belief that it could prescribe an agenda for assimilating into the larger population those who had been brought to America in chains and subjugated, first as slaves and then as second-class citizens, for close to two centuries. In today's political and economic climate it is hard to remember how seriously that responsibility was taken in the late 1960s. The middle years of the decade had seen an explosion of civil-rights laws and court decisions intended to unshackle blacks in the South, in the wake of which it was considered likely that the nation would give blacks the same kind of mobility and economic opportunity that other minority groups had achieved over several generations.

As the commission neared the end of its work, in February of 1968, there was a sense of excitement and anticipation about its forthcoming report, sharpened by rumors that liberals and conservatives on the commission were divided on what the report should say. I was promised a copy of the Kerner Report three days in advance of its release. But no sooner had I gotten a copy and set up interviews with members of the commission and staff than another newspaper, claiming to have obtained a copy from unofficial sources, announced it was breaking the release date for both print and broadcast. I was left with less than three hours to digest the voluminous report and summarize what it said in order to make the *Times* deadline.

I did the best I could, writing mostly from the commission's summary of the report. Other newspapers and broadcasters were in the same difficult situation, and it was from those hurriedly written accounts that the American people first learned of the report's conclusions: that there was no conspiracy to destroy the cities, but that the riots were spontaneous outbursts of protest against conditions in the ghettos, often made more severe by unnecessary police violence. Yet so strong was the interest in the Kerner Report that stories appeared for weeks afterward, and more than a million copies of the report were sold. Meetings of government officials and citizen groups were held in cities and suburbs across the nation to decide how they should react to the report.

Whatever disagreements there were on the use of such language as "Our nation is moving toward two societies, one black, one white—separate and unequal," the Kerner Report was in keeping with the thought of millions of well-informed Americans of both races. Nor was the liberal Establishment of the day jarred by the further observation of the commission:

> *What white Americans have never fully understood—but what the Negro can never forget—is that white society is deeply implicated in the ghetto. White institutions created it, white institutions maintain it, and white society condones it.*

Such language could just as well have rolled off the tongue of the President of the United States to a national television audience. President Johnson had been making similar statements for a long time, even prior to his election to office in 1964. Nor were the commission's recommendations for government action, though ambitious and extensive, considered radical. Mostly they were extensions of what the federal government already was doing on a broad front of social and economic assistance to the disadvantaged.

The severity of the riots, little remembered by most Americans, certainly called for more than a routine response. Between 1965 and 1969, when the disorders began to taper off, about 250 persons were killed—far more than died in two decades of nonviolent protests in the South—12,000 were injured, 83,000 were arrested, and property damage totaled hundreds of millions of dollars, according to various estimates. On July 27, 1967, when President Johnson announced that he would appoint a commission, Detroit was in flames and under army occupation and much of Newark was in ruins; in that month forty cities from San Francisco to Buffalo were beset by burning, breaking, looting, and warring with the police. White liberals huddled in suburbs and cities across the country to discuss what they could do.

The Kerner Report was dated March 1, 1968. A new wave of riots soon erupted, the assassination of Dr. Martin Luther King, Jr., on April 4; following the spread of violence and burning reached to within a few blocks of the White House, where armed Marines were stationed to prevent any damage to the building or grounds. One of the most remarkable aspects of the commission's work was extensive surveys, published several months after the release of the main report, of rioters and other blacks living in the central cities. The surveys showed that the majority considered the rioting not criminal acts by youth gangs—as much of the white community believed—but legitimate protests about the abysmal conditions in which black urban residents lived. Implicit in this belief was another: that the white society would find the rioting so intolerable that it would move as it never had to remedy conditions. To me, this meant that the "American dream" of equality and justice for all was internalized, not only among those groups who had been assimilated into the prospering majority but by the most unfortunate of those still excluded.

The riots eventually stopped as the police became more sophisticated and learned how to head them off, and as local and national black leaders, seeing the enormous damage and the unlikelihood of corrective action by the federal government, called for an end to that kind of social protest.

President Johnson's coolness to the report, which had in fact been deliberately designed to find remedies of the kind he would approve, was blamed by some on his pique that it did not give him enough credit for what he had already done for blacks. But the cause went much deeper than that. It was a presidential-election year. National attention was shifting away from domestic problems to the Vietnam War and its drain on the economy, as well as to war-inspired protests and student revolts against authority on college campuses. Politicians were beginning to be aware of a white backlash, in which ethnic groups were bitterly complaining that blacks had received more than their share of government money and legal assistance. There was widespread fear of violent crime, robbery, and burglary, with poor blacks receiving much of the blame. Even Vice-President Hubert H. Humphrey, who was running for president with Lyndon Johnson's blessings, turned cool on the Kerner Report after first praising it. The report was thus filed away to gather dust in the archives as

America tried to forget about the riots and the troubled ghettos.

But the distress in the central cities did not go away. Ten years later, after I had completed a tour as an editor in Washington and New York and returned to writing, I was asked to do the lead story on a series marking the tenth anniversary of the report and whatever impact it may have had on the country. It was a difficult assignment, in part because many Americans had forgotten that there ever was a Kerner Report and many others considered it a symbol of what were termed "excesses" of liberal domestic programs of the Kennedy and Johnson administrations.

I sent questionnaires to *Times* stringers in cities across the country asking them to find out through extensive reporting and interviewing what had happened in their communities in the intervening ten years, and traveled to a number of cities myself to gather information. The story I filed said in part that in 1978:

> *A majority of the members of the Commission that produced the controversial report, many white students of America's racial struggles and a large body of black and white leaders on the national and community levels believe that the prophesy of division has been at least partially borne out by events and that a reversal of the trend would be more difficult now than in that tumultuous year which saw violent upheavals over race, politics and the Vietnam war.*
>
> *In their view, the present and future are more bleak for millions remaining in what the Commission called the urban ghettos; blacks who have left in substantial numbers for better lives elsewhere are caught up increasingly in middle-class concerns and are no longer active in the cause of those left behind;*

and the majority of whites, now more isolated from the slums than they were a decade ago, believe that discrimination has ended and there is no racial problem remaining.

This view of developments, combined with the fact of chronically high unemployment in the ghettos, in good times and bad, has raised fears that the nation may have acquired a permanent underclass, wards of the government living out unproductive lives under conditions that most Americans consider unacceptable.

My report pointed out that almost everyone concerned acknowledged that the nation's 25 million blacks as a whole had made considerable gains over the decade. Many urban blacks, perhaps 30 percent, had worked their way into the middle class and moved to the suburbs or to better housing within the cities. And many still dependent on public assistance had received a substantial increase in real income through rent subsidies, a liberalized food-stamp plan, and other benefits enacted since 1968. The number of black officials had increased dramatically. Blacks had moved up in business, television, and sports. The Kerner Commission found it appalling in 1968 that there were virtually no blacks in Establishment journalism. And I can testify that it was the commission's recommendation that caused newspapers like my own to hire their first black reporters and editors.

Yet the commission was concerned chiefly with those large concentrations of poor urban blacks. And for them, conditions described in the report had worsened by 1978, and the boundaries of the ghettos had spread.

Now, after another ten years, the black ghettos are still there and new horrors have arrived for many of the victims: homelessness, increased use of drugs, and the spread of AIDS, even to children, partly as a result of infected needles used to inject the drugs. Also, the ghettos have spread far beyond their 1968 or 1978 borders.

Reporters like to bring statistics to life with their own observations. Over the past decade I have observed that affluent whites, along with some affluent blacks and other racial minorities, have moved farther and farther into the distant suburbs and exurbs, chasing the office parks and other places of employment along the freeways and leaving the urban ghettos more isolated than ever from mainstream, prospering Americans. Within the cities, welfare dependency has become even more institutionalized than it was in 1968 or 1978, as factory jobs and others requiring little education have been replaced by jobs requiring more specialized skills that ghetto residents lack. The working middle class that once made up the vast majority of city dwellers has left the cities in great numbers. Lawyers, accountants, stockbrokers, people in advertising, and other professionals and their support staffs occupy those shiny new office buildings, and the result is great, ostentatious wealth beside dismal, spreading poverty.

I have found over the years that it is dangerous to predict what may happen in the future in America, which is ever volatile. But there may be some small glimmers of hope here and there. One is that—and who would ever have expected it after eight years of the Reagan administration?—there is renewed interest in the subjects addressed by the Kerner Commission. In February 1988 alone, I was invited to three conferences concerned with the twenty-year-old Kerner Report and its impact. I have found also that if the business of America is business, as Calvin Coolidge declared, it may be good news that many business leaders are moving away from the staunch conservatism that marked their political philosophy in the past. Part of this has to do with the international economy that has come to America over the past few years. There is a growing realization among both political and business leaders that communities with many poorly educated, destitute people cannot compete for industries and services that demand highly skilled workers. Business leaders more and more are joining political leaders in pressing the support for education, and even welfare, when it promises to make people self-supporting in the long run.

I find the glimmer of hope to lie here, in coalitions between political and business leaders, because I am convinced that at no time in the foreseeable future will the federal government come up with a national policy of curbing poverty and abuses in the central cities. Over a period of three decades, even before it was restrained by budget deficits, the federal government has proved itself incapable of doing so, and the responsibility for making changes that would lead to the assimilation of poor blacks now lies with state and local government. At its best, the national government can, as it should, provide a uniform minimum welfare payment. The innovations needed for transforming the urban ghettos, however, must come, at least initially, from some other level of government or from the private sector.

There is precedent for business bringing about social change. In the final analysis, the South succumbed to racial desegregation not so much because of federal law but because to do so was considered good for business. After the state and local defiance in the Little Rock school desegregation crisis, it was seven years before the community could attract new industrial plants. Industrialists and businesses across the South saw that failure to comply with desegregation laws meant a loss of business income. It is no less plausible that business leaders may find that the urban ghettos should no longer be tolerated because their presence is not good for business. There already is a trend in this direction in a number of states and regions where business leaders have joined with public officials in demanding improvements in education and other basic social services, even when tax increases are needed to pay for them. As many black leaders said in the South during the 1960s, it is change itself that is important to oppressed people, not so much how or why it occurs.

Part II

TODAY'S WORSENED POVERTY

"Pervasive unemployment and underemployment are the most persistent and serious grievances in minority areas," the Kerner Report declared. Unfortunately, unemployment and poverty are worse now in America—for everybody—than they were twenty years ago.

More Americans are poor today (32.4 million in 1986, 13.6 percent of the population) than were poor twenty years ago (24 million in 1969, 12.1 percent of the population). David Hamilton points out in Chapter 3 that the fact that we seem to rediscover poverty every so often does not prove that it must always be with us. To the contrary, Hamilton shows that America has both the technological and the economic means to eliminate poverty altogether. The fact that we do not do so, he asserts, is partly a result of our cultural beliefs and myths that justify the wealth of the rich as deserved, and condemns the poverty of the poor as both inevitable and their own fault.

In Chapter 4, Gary D. Sandefur shows, too, that poverty is worse, pointing out that while poverty has decreased for the elderly since the Kerner Report, it has increased for children, both minority and nonminority. Like the Kerner Commission, he believes that America must fight poverty wherever it is—no less in rural areas than in the cities, no less among whites than among blacks and other minorities. Sandefur makes clear that a number of federal programs, some of which have fallen into disfavor or have been abandoned, actually were successful—including Aid to Families with Dependent Children (AFDC), public-service employment, job training, affirmative action, and community health centers. Sandefur's findings about programs that worked point toward renewed federal efforts along these and related lines.

CHAPTER 3

Poverty Is Still With Us—and Worse

DAVID HAMILTON

POVERTY, FOR TWO hundred years at least, has been a consistent part of the "American way of life"—always there, but always obscured by what Richard Parker calls "the myth of the middle class." Every so often the myth, somewhat like a great fog, lifts, and the reality of poverty is discovered once again. Perhaps the notoriety of the homeless today may be one of those liftings. When a homeless person seeks shelter in a dumpster and gets compacted inside a refuse truck, as recently happened in Albuquerque, it is hard indeed to ignore the sensational poverty level.[1] That kind of event attracts the attention of the press in a manner that the poor, merely exercising their right to sleep under bridges not for the moment occupied by the rich, just do not get.

The poor are rediscovered every twenty years or so. Between times, myth usually prevails over fact. This was most certainly true just before the rediscovery of poverty in the 1960s, true before its overwhelming visibility in the 1930s, and most certainly true in the late 1970s and most of the 1980s. So it was one hundred years ago.

The so-called Gay Nineties were anything but gay for those at the bottom end of the social ladder. As Otto L. Bettman wrote in the opening paragraphs of *The Good Old Days—They Were Terrible*:

> *But this gaiety was only a brittle veneer that covered widespread turmoil and suffering. The good old days were good for but the privileged few. For the farmer, the laborer, the average breadwinner, life was an unremitting hardship. This segment of the population was exploited or lived in the shadow of total neglect.* [2]

Bettman is talking about a larger segment of the population than that with which we associate poverty, but his book makes clear that, for many, the level of living was far below that of the average worker of the time. During the same period of which Bettman was writing, Henry George graphically noted in his *Progress and Poverty* that in the midst of all the technical progress of the late nineteenth century, an impoverished way of life continued to exist.[3]

In the 1920s, the United States was agog over Prohibition, bootleg liquor, the flapper, keeping cool with Coolidge, and a new permanent plateau of prosperity. A fog seemed to obscure the poverty of the black sharecropper, the farmer faced with a heavy mortgage and falling farm prices, the migrant agricultural workers (tramps) studied by Paul Taylor, and the southern textile workers, and most certainly it never allowed even a peep at the plight of the American Indians. Although much of what was roaring in the twenties is now known to have been a figment of the imagination, the fog was so thick, that even today it is the myth that is most frequently portrayed in television reconstructions.

In the next decade, with one-third of a nation in obvious poverty, the matter could not be obscured. The homeless, building permanent shelters in Central Park, demanded attention.[4] Americans admitted that there was a "poverty way of life" that was an integral part of the "American way of life." But after World War II and the immediate postwar concern over worldwide poverty, the fog again descended in the form of the "affluent society" doctrine.

According to the conventional wisdom of the time, America had a well-developed welfare state, which consisted of the New Deal's income-maintenance programs. These were all financed by a progressive income tax, which, when taken in conjunction with the welfare measures, meant that the rich had been reduced to a level of living that was being rapidly approached by the rising poor. And it was a meaningful transfer of income, because as productive capacity expanded during World War II real per-capita income had increased startlingly.

This was a belief so firmly held that writers like David Reisman and Joseph Wood Krutch sounded an alarm over the uniformity that was overtaking the American way of life.[5] Distinctions of taste were being lost. As a matter of fact, the threat was becoming worldwide. As American abundance and largesse passed on to the rest of the world, the unwary beneficiaries were about to be "coca-colaized."

The rediscovery of poverty in the 1960s is usually attributed to a political campaign and some coincidental literary events. President Kennedy is alleged to have seen the whites of poverty's eyes in the hills and hollows of West Virginia in the course of a political campaign. Then in 1962, several books—by Michael Harrington, Gabriel Kolko, James Morgan, and others, as well as Dwight MacDonald's *New Yorker* review of Harrington—helped Kennedy's West Virginia revelation to lift the affluent-society fog.[6] Whether this is a correct interpretation or not, such a fog could not possibly have withstood the events of the middle of the decade. Most of the time, those who experience poverty do so with decorum and decency. They do not call attention to their presence. When they do so, however, it is apt to be explosive, as in the middle sixties.

But even these protests were soon superseded by the largely middle-class protests over Vietnam. Once again, the poor disappeared. Throughout the 1970s and 1980s, we were treated to the alleged excesses of the welfare state.[7] Only the homeless threatened to disrupt the "benign neglect" with which poverty was handled in this decade of Reagan and the one that preceded it—an almost twenty-year stretch during which the fear of inflation was so great that poverty (unemployment) was used as a major weapon to offset it.

In between fogs, when we have been able to see the level of poverty in our midst, our interpretation of the causes of poverty has affected what we have done about it. Prior to the 1930s, our interpretations were largely, but not exclusively, individualistic, and the settlement houses, and the earlier thrift movements, were typical solutions. Private charity was to be preferred to public. Moral exhortation was common, and flawed character was blamed.[8]

None of this holds, of course, for Marxists and other "radicals" who always interpreted poverty as a social phenomenon endemic to capitalism, and an essential element of capital accumulation that would intensify as capitalism matured. This view held that reformers who thought poverty might be ameliorated were actually traitors to the poor, for it was only by poverty's intensification that capitalism would eventually be brought down, after which the poor would inherit the earth. Within American officialdom and among the populace at large, such ideas were ignored much as poverty was ignored. The official view was that poverty was a product of some individual lacking, and that, since individual lacking, like original sin, was always present, poverty would be too.

Not until the 1930s was there any seriousness about treating poverty through some substantial changes in the social order. With one-third of a nation "ill fed, ill housed, and ill clothed," a contention that their plight was attributable to moral turpitude was rather unconvincing. How could anyone convincingly argue that between 1929 and 1933 some 11 million individuals, formerly employed, developed serious character flaws? The problem of poverty was never so clearly seen to be a social rather than an individual one.

Nothing so radical as Beveridge's security "from the cradle to the grave" was advocated by the New Deal. But the New Deal did address the matter of income maintenance to reduce the insecurities of an industrial economy. Although an industrial economy is by most measures more secure than earlier economies, it does have a major insecurity induced by inadequate aggregate demand. Mass unemployment and, hence, mass poverty follow, as was only too apparent in the 1930s. But insecurity can also occur for any number of other reasons: industrial accidents, death of an income-earning parent, retirement and old age, and noncyclical unemployment. These the New Deal recognized, and, in response, it either strengthened existing legislation and programs or created wholly new ones. But the aim of these programs was to maintain a minimum stream of income. They were not intended to eliminate poverty.

That the New Deal "welfare state" neither could nor intended to eliminate poverty was obscured in the 1950s by the "affluent society" myth. The belief that the New Deal had massively shifted income distribution in favor of low-income receivers was an essential part of the larger myth. Content with the notion that all Americans now lived on easy street, the nation was indeed shocked when the 1960 census revealed otherwise.

With more than 39 million people—22 percent of the population—living below the poverty line in 1960, one could hardly argue that the society was affluent. The famous 1964 *Economic Report of the President* contained the first official recognition of poverty as a major American problem. It noted the same bleak picture revealed by the earlier census data.

> *There were 47 million families in the United States in 1962. Fully 9.3 million, or one-fifth of these families—comprising more than 30 million persons—had total money income below $3,000. More than 11 million of these family members were children, one-sixth of our youth. . . . Thus, by the measures used here, 33 to 35 million Americans were living at or below the boundaries of poverty in 1962—nearly one-fifth of our nation.* [9]

In 1964, war was declared on poverty—not a large war, mind you, but one with the expressed goal of eliminating poverty by the symbolic year 1976. That this was never a big war is evident from the expenditure of less than $2 billion a year at its height. Meanwhile, the *really* big war in Vietnam was budgeted for more than ten times that amount.

But the significance of the "war on poverty" was what appeared to be an attitudinal change in government policy, as well as a change in the will to do something to eliminate that seemingly permanent part of the American way of life. Always in the past, in the nineteenth century and earlier in this one, only "dreamers" had conjured up a society in which poverty no longer was an accepted feature. Not only was poverty's elimination declared official policy, but the 1964 *Economic Report* noted that it would take an expenditure of only $11 billion to bring all families and individuals then below the poverty line up to that minimal standard: "Conquest of poverty is well within our power."[10] To appreciate that this was no exaggeration, note that America's gross national product grew by $55 billion in 1965 alone. One-fifth of that growth, if appropriated for the poor, would have eliminated all officially defined poverty in the country.

What is ironic is that it took us almost forty years to recognize what a Brookings Institution study called *The Distribution of Wealth and Income in Relation to Economic Progress* had clearly demonstrated about the capability of the American economy in the 1920s. The study examined the performance of the American economy in the second half of the not-so-roaring twenties. In one volume, *America's Capacity to Produce,* it showed that in the late 1920s the industrial sector of the American economy operated at 80 percent of capacity.[11] The second volume, *America's Capacity to Consume,* showed that had the additional 20 percent of capacity been used and the additional income distributed to the lowest-income receivers, no family would have had less than $2,000 in 1929. ($14,561 in 1988 dollars).[12]

It must also be emphasized that those estimates were based on the industrial capability of the 1925–29 industrial economy—not on the much greater industrial capability of the 1988 economy. America has had the technological capability to eliminate all poverty for at least sixty years.

Although the "war on poverty" represented a wholly new attitude toward the possibility of eliminating poverty instead of ameliorating it, it still resembled the individualistic approach of the pre–New Deal days. The authors of the "war" were greatly affected by the notion that the New Deal income-maintenance programs had been unsuccessful in doing something they were never designed to do—eliminate poverty. They had been in place in some form for twenty-five years, and lo and behold, poverty was still with us. Like today's conservatives, they claimed that the programs themselves tended to perpetuate poverty.

Since the 1964 *Economic Report* had said that only $11 billion would get everyone up to the poverty line, one might have expected suggestions now for raising benefits under the existing maintenance programs. Instead, nineteenth-century notions of personal betterment were resurrected. No one mentioned flawed character as the root of the problem, but flawed productive capabilities were said to be prominent causes of poverty. Children were given Head Start, adults were trained for jobs and taught basic skills, and ghetto occupants received training and organization to represent their interests at city hall. Once trained, it was thought, the poor would cross the poverty line under their own steam.

Whatever the reason—the war on poverty, the tax cut and drop in unemployment, or the additional expenditures for Vietnam—serious inroads on poverty had clearly been made by 1969. The poverty population had been reduced by about one-third, from 36 million in 1964 to only slightly over 24 million in 1969. The percentage of the population living below the poverty line had fallen from 19 percent to 12.1 percent.

TABLE 3.1 NUMBER AND PERCENT OF PEOPLE BELOW THE POVERTY LEVEL, 1986

Characteristic	Number	Percent
ALL PERSONS	**32,370,000**	**13.6**
White	22,183,000	11.0
Black	8,983,000	31.1
Hispanic	5,117,000	27.3
Under 15 years	11,018,000	21.2
15 to 24 years	5,991,000	16.0
25 to 44 years	7,815,000	10.2
45 to 54 years	1,886,000	8.2
55 to 59 years	1,113,000	10.0
60 to 64 years	1,071,000	9.9
65 years and over	3,477,000	12.4
Northeast	5,211,000	10.5
Midwest	7,641,000	13.0
South	13,106,000	16.1
West	6,412,000	13.2
ALL RELATED CHILDREN UNDER EIGHTEEN YEARS IN FAMILIES	**12,257,000**	**19.8**
White	7,714,000	15.3
Black	4,039,000	42.7
Hispanic	2,413,000	37.1
ALL FAMILIES	**7,023,000**	**10.9**
White	4,811,000	8.6
Black	1,987,000	28.0
Hispanic	1,085,000	24.7
Married-couple families	3,123,000	6.1
Male householder, no wife present	287,000	11.4
Female householder, no husband present	3,613,000	34.6
ALL UNRELATED INDIVIDUALS	**6,846,000**	**21.6**
Male	2,536,000	17.5
Female	4,311,000	25.1

Source: U.S. Bureau of the Census, *Money Income and Poverty Status of Families and Persons in the United States, 1986*, pp. 5–6.

One might have taken heart and actually hoped that the 1976 goal would be met. But, of course, no such achievement could be celebrated when the tall ships came into New York Harbor that year. In 1976, poverty was still the way of life for almost 25 million Americans, 11.8 percent of the population. And by that time, poverty had once again become an unmentionable. From 1979 through 1986, the poverty level stayed above 13 percent, climbing as high as 15.2 percent in 1983. More than 33 million Americans were poor in 1983; great progress was claimed when the total dropped marginally in 1986, below 32.5 million. Twenty years after the Kerner Report, the United States has neither eliminated nor reduced the poverty level. Table 3.1 might well be labeled, "Same Song, Second Verse."

At the time of the 1960s rediscovery of poverty, its profile was much as it remains today, though of course some proportions have changed. Female-headed households now make up a sizable proportion of the poverty population, which certainly contributes to the fact that almost one out of five children lives below the poverty line. Harrell Rogers calls this phenomenon "the feminization of poverty."[13] Though a catchy term, it obscures the fact that the other elements that were once prominent in the poverty profile, while reduced proportionately, are still there.

The South—a large part of the "flourishing" Sun Belt—contains the highest incidence of poverty, while the Northeast, a large part of the Rust Belt, has the lowest. But no region has a monopoly hold on the nation's poor. So it was, twenty years ago. Poverty then was nationwide, and so it is today.

About two-thirds of the poor population is white, and that has not changed significantly. Blacks and Hispanics, on the other hand, both have a significantly higher incidence of poverty than do whites. That too was true twenty years ago.

The one American group that has shown remarkable change within the poverty profile is composed of those sixty-five and older. They were well over one-fourth of the poor population in the 1960s, with a poverty incidence of around 30 percent. Today, the incidence is down to 12.4 percent. While this is higher than that for all age categories between twenty-five and sixty-four years, it does mean that the threat of poverty at and after age sixty-five is less severe than it once was. Most of this improvement is attributed to a more effective Social Security system, which seems to indicate that "Problems cannot be solved by throwing money at them" is just too glib a statement. It is apparently possible to increase money benefits to the aged without debauching them, something that conservatives, for some strange reason, apparently feel is not possible with people at other age levels.

But even in regard to this seemingly marked improvement among the elderly, some cautious observations must be made, as Michael Harrington has done. He contends that the improved condition of the seniors is a precarious one. For one thing, it is contingent on a well-managed economy—one that provides for the full employment of younger people.

> *But if the American economy continues to malfunction for another decade or so, it could well be that some unscrupulous politician will notice the figures that so intrigued Peter Peterson [former Secretary of Commerce]. When asked why he robbed banks, Willie Sutton said, "Because that's where the money is." And if a reactionary politician looks around for cuts, his eye will eventually alight upon Social Security. Because that's where most of the social spending is.* [14]

Furthermore, the lot of many senior citizens has been only marginally improved by Social Security. It would not take a very large cut in benefits to push a substantial number of older Americans below the poverty line again.

Noting the persistence of poverty, however, leads one too easily to the notion that nothing can be done: that the problem is really not a problem; it is just a part of life. But for all the cynicism of the policymakers, it is really not characteristic of the American outlook on social matters to simply write problems off. It seems to me more characteristic for Americans to view such sticky problems as challenges.

And the challenge is not to lament the elusiveness of an answer, but to ask why a nation with the industry and technology to eliminate poverty persistently failed to do so. Most certainly, the problem is not one of lacking the means. Our problem is an institutional one; it is not a technological one. In one sense the problem is sociological, not economic.

We have a reluctance to view our culture as coolly as we view the cultures that have been studied by anthropologists. When the Mafalu Mountain Folk of Papua, for example, refuse to increase their output of taros by using hoes instead of digging sticks, because they fear that iron hoes will poison the soil, we note this as an unfounded fear that impedes their progress. But we Americans, it is said, live in a culture of reason; we have no such cultural hangups.

In fact, as Walter Goldschmidt has pointed out, we are but one culture among others.[15] We can, indeed, analyze our culture in the same matter-of-fact way that we study other peoples. And if we are to understand the persistence of poverty within a culture with the technological capability of eliminating it, it is on that level of generalization that we must proceed.

All peoples have a system of status-ranking, of grades and

ratings based on some putative difference of social worth.[16] This ranking system is not of people *per se*; rather, it is of the roles that they play. This attribution of *mana*, as the Polynesians put it, to explain the deferential manner in which people in high positions are approached has a negative side: those who are in inferior positions may, if they associate too closely with those in higher positions, actually profane them. Thus the Brahmins of India avoided the "untouchables." Apparently, it was this same kind of belief that segregated America's swimming pools and other public facilities not too long ago: a ritual pollution was feared, not a physiological or biological one. Today's American poor are in a similar kind of social limbo.

Role behavior in any culture is scrupulously defined by mores and taboos. We behave differently toward our father's brother than toward our father. We behave one way with the president of the university, another with a fellow professor, and yet another with our students. It takes a while to learn this role behavior, which is based upon a set of reinforcing beliefs, a mixture of fact and myth.

As Veblen insisted in the very first chapter of *The Theory of the Leisure Class*, income distribution follows the lines of the status system: those in high positions are credited with great prowess in contributing to the general welfare; it is therefore only right and good that they should enjoy the rather generous fruits of their contribution. They are then compelled to put their wealth on show in the forms of conspicuous consumption and conspicuous leisure. This presupposes, of course, the relative lack of consumption and leisure in other segments of the population.

In *The Social Foundations of British Wage Policy*, the eminent English economist Barbara Wootton showed very effectively how the status system in Great Britain preserved

TABLE 3.2 INCOME DISTRIBUTION

Population Group, by Income	Percent of Total Income					
	1947	1950	1960	1967	1984	1985
Highest fifth	43.0	42.6	42.0	41.2	42.9	43.5
Fourth fifth	23.1	23.5	23.6	23.7	24.4	24.6
Middle fifth	17.0	17.4	17.6	17.5	17.0	16.9
Second fifth	11.8	12.0	12.0	12.2	11.0	10.9
Lowest fifth	5.0	4.5	4.9	5.4	4.7	4.6
Top 40%	66.1	66.1	65.6	64.9	67.3	68.1
Bottom 40%	16.8	16.5	16.9	17.6	15.7	15.5

Source: U.S. Bureau of the Census, *Statistical Abstract of the United States, 1969, 1986, 1987.*

a long-standing relative distribution of income.[17] As she found, the relative distribution of wages among the British work force between the 1930s and the 1950s showed remarkable rigidity; although in real terms the remuneration for most occupations had gone up, relative to one another they pretty much remained the same. The social ranking of the work roles had remained essentially the same and had only changed in rather close unison.

No comparable study has been done of wage allocation in the United States, but the fragmentary data that does exist indicates that income distribution here has not changed radically (see Table 3.2). The stability of income distribution throughout the decade of the 1950s would indicate that any income shift suggested by the term *affluent society* was not readily apparent. A minutely narrower gap in distribution in 1967 may show some of the effects of the "war on poverty" or of a falling unemployment rate. The two years, 1984 and

1985, in the midst of the Reagan administration, showed the widest gap between those at the top and those at the bottom. Still, the numbers indicate stability rather than significant change.

Robert Holman, in his *Poverty: Explanations of Social Deprivation,* primarily about England, argues that poverty is a function of a stratified society, of a system of status.[18] And, as such, it performs the function of justifying the riches of the rich. If poverty can be said to be attributable to the slackness and lack of moral fiber of the poor, then the riches of the rich are justified on the basis of moral fiber, hard work, and diligence. The rich are rich because of their greater productivity and contribution to social well-being. The same would seem to hold for the United States.

The beliefs that shape a system are held by both their beneficiaries and those who might best be called its victims. The poor are often as convinced of their unworthiness as the rich are. In our own culture, the major justification for poverty is the productivity argument of the economist: the poor are poor because they are less productive; the rich are rich because they are extremely productive; and all incomes reflect the relative productivity of the recipients. Yet, strange as it may seem, we have no independent measure of whatever "productivity" is other than the wage paid. The high income paid to the manufacturer of poison gas, cigarettes, or Saturday-night specials," or to the writer of advertising, is in fact the measure of the social worth of that individual's contribution to the total product. And the absence of income on the part of the poor is evidence of their unworthiness.

Of course, we hear other arguments today, too, to justify poverty, such as the belief that the poor, because of their slovenly ways, inflict a life of poverty on themselves.[19] Other justifications are more substantial, such as the notion that the poor are unable to postpone immediate gratification. Actually, their incomes are such as to stifle any kind of gratification. (It is not the poor who keep the RV industry going, but those whose income is somewhat higher, who have access to credit, and thus can yield most readily to instant gratification.) And another current argument proposes that the poor are poor because they lack a penchant for risk-taking. Since risk-taking is supposedly the road to riches, and its absence is poverty, the whole dubious proposition says no more than that the poor remain poor because they are afraid of becoming rich.

But poverty in the midst of plenty will continue so long as the beliefs that justify it continue unchallenged. The myths that justify poverty, as well as the myths that gloss it over, must go if that level of living is to disappear from the American way of life. That will require a revolution, not only among the populace at large, but among the intellectuals, the makers and shapers of ideas. But unfortunately, from that quarter we have recently had an outpouring of so-called studies that reinforce the conventional wisdom.[20] In this light we can better appreciate the significance of the 1964 *Economic Report of the President.* The concluding paragraph of the report's chapter on poverty stated:

> *The Nation's attack on poverty must be based on a change in attitude. We must open our eyes and minds to the poverty in our midst. Poverty is not the inevitable fate of any man. The condition can be eradicated; and since it can be, it must be. It is time to renew our faith in the worth and capacity of all human beings; . . . and to allow Government to assume its responsibility for action and leadership in promoting the general welfare.*[21]

That sounds grandiloquent today. And so it was. But it contains a major nugget of truth. Without such a change, twenty or even sixty years from now the poverty level will remain unchanged within this major industrial nation. (The other exhortation possible is that of revolution. But that route does not have a very good track record. It is rather like burning down the house to get roast pig.) But twenty years after the Kerner Report, twenty-four years after the 1964 *Economic Report,* America is still inhibited by a philosophy that considers poverty inevitable and simultaneously blames the poor for their plight. And, if we persist in such a fog, the "fire next time" could be even more devastating than it was twenty years ago.

CHAPTER 4

Blacks, Hispanics, American Indians, and Poverty—and What Worked

GARY D. SANDEFUR

THE PURPOSE OF the Kerner Commission was not specifically to examine poverty among urban blacks, but to examine circumstances behind the riots that had broken out in major urban areas of the United States in the late 1960s. In his charge to the Kerner Commission, President Johnson stated:

> *We need to know the answers, I think, to three questions about these riots:*
>
> ... What happened?
>
> ... Why did it happen?
>
> ... What can be done to prevent it from happening again and again?

To answer the second and third questions, the commission examined the prevalence, causes, and possible solutions to poverty in urban areas, especially among central-city blacks.

Among the commission's conclusions was that the segregation and poverty of black ghettos were two of the major forces leading to riots and other forms of violence. The report carefully documented the extent of poverty in urban areas. Using 1964 data from the Social Security Administration, the commission reported that 30.7 percent of nonwhite families and 8.8 percent of white families were below the poverty line. Further, 43.6 percent of the poor in central cities were nonwhite and 26 percent of nonwhite families in central cities had female heads. Among female-headed families, the prevalence of poverty was twice as high as among male-headed families, and 81 percent of children under six living in nonwhite, female-headed families were poor. It is frustrating and saddening that these comparisons of blacks and whites and the relatively poor situation of inner-city blacks continue to be true in contemporary American society.

My purpose here is to survey the current situation of poor minorities in the inner city and in the United States in general in light of the findings and recommendations of the Kerner Report. I will first review the commission's findings and conclusions about poverty among minority groups in urban areas, and then examine changes in poverty, and developments in social policy, since the report was first issued.

URBAN POVERTY IN THE 1960s

The Kerner Report documented a sad and serious picture of poverty and disadvantage in the central cities of the United States. This assessment was balanced, however, by the gains that blacks had made during the 1960s. Relying on figures from the Departments of Labor and Commerce, the commission reported that the incomes of blacks and whites were rising, the size of the black upper-income group was expanding rapidly, and the size of the lowest-income group had decreased. There remained, on the other hand, a considerable group of blacks who did not appear to be benefiting from economic gains, including a group of 2 million "hard core disadvantaged" in central cities. Black unemployment rates were double those of whites, and the most disadvantaged working blacks were concentrated in the least desirable and rewarding jobs. The report stated that "in disadvantaged areas, employment conditions for blacks are in a chronic state of crisis."[1] These contradictory and complex themes of progress by some blacks, contrasted with hopelessness and despair for others, continue to be reflected in contemporary discussions of disadvantage and poverty. For example, in *The Declining Significance of Race* (1978), William Julius Wilson argued that some blacks were benefiting from the growing openness of American society while others were being left behind. He develops this theme further in his 1987 book *The Truly Disadvantaged.*

The Kerner Report attempted to assess the causes and consequences of poverty among central-city blacks. Again, its conclusions are reflected in contemporary discussions of these problems. The report stated that "a close correlation exists between the number of nonwhite married women separated from their husbands each year and the unemployment rate among nonwhite males 20 years old and over," and "the proportion of fatherless families appears to be increasing in the poorest Negro neighborhoods."[2] Recent analysts have focused on black male unemployment as a major factor in the high incidence of black females as heads of families.[3] The report identified changes in the American economy, including decreased demand for unskilled labor in central cities, as major factors in black unemployment.

The Kerner Report concluded that the nation was moving rapidly toward two increasingly separate Americas and that immediate and long-term actions should be taken to prevent this from happening. The report suggested a number of policy changes, which I will review later.

CENTRAL-CITY AND MINORITY POVERTY SINCE 1968

Since the late 1960s, the number of poor people living in the central city has increased dramatically, as has the proportion of the central-city population that is poor. In 1969 12.7 percent (8 million people) of the central-city population was poor, whereas 19.9 percent (12.7 million) of this population was poor in 1982; in 1985, 19 percent (14.2 million Americans) of the central-city population was poor.[4] Wilson attributes this increase in both the prevalence of poverty and the numbers of inner-city poor to changes that have taken place in the economies of metropolitan areas. In the past,

TABLE 4.1 PERCENTAGES OF INDIVIDUALS BELOW THE POVERTY LINE, BY YEAR, 1959–85

Group	1959	1969	1979	1985
A. ALL PERSONS				
White	18.1	9.5	9.0	11.4
Black	55.1	32.2	31.0	31.3
Hispanic	NA	NA	21.8	29.0
Native American	NA	38.3	27.5	NA
B. PERSONS IN HOUSEHOLDS WITH FEMALE HEADS				
White	40.2	29.1	25.2	29.8
Black	70.6	58.2	53.1	53.2
Hispanic	NA	NA	51.2	55.7
Native American	NA	63.5	46.4	NA
C. RELATED CHILDREN UNDER EIGHTEEN IN FAMILIES [a]				
White	20.6	9.7	11.4	15.6
Black	65.6	39.6	40.8	43.1
Hispanic	NA	NA	27.7	39.6
Native American	NA	44.9	32.2	NA
D. PERSONS SIXTY-FIVE AND OVER				
White	33.1	23.3	13.3	11.0
Black	62.5	50.2	36.2	31.5
Hispanic	NA	NA	26.8	23.9
Native American	NA	50.8	32.1	NA

Source: U.S. Bureau of the Census, *Poverty in the United States: 1985,* Tables 1 and 2; *1980 Census: General Social and Economic Characteristics,* Table 129; *1970 Census: American Indians; 1970 Census: Low Income Population.*

[a]Refers to children living in families in which they are related to the householder.

NA: Data not available.

there were jobs in central cities for people with no skills and little education, but this is no longer true. Furthermore, people with skills and education have fled the ghetto, so that the central-city population is disproportionately young, uneducated, unskilled, and poor. The lack of a middle class in the central cities has led to the social isolation of those lower-class individuals who have been left behind. Their social isolation leads to inadequate ties to the job market and generates behavior that is not conducive to good work histories.

The focus of the Kerner Report and Wilson's work on the conditions in the central cities can be better interpreted in light of trends in poverty in general. Poverty rates are actually higher now than in 1968 for a number of groups. Table 4.1 shows poverty rates for selected population groups in 1959 through 1985. These statistics indicate that the United States made dramatic progress in reducing poverty during the 1960s among all sectors of the population represented in the table, but little or no progress since the Kerner Report. In addition, as Adams, Duncan, and Rodgers show (see Chapter 5), poverty has become more persistent since the mid-1970s—that is, the chances of a poor person escaping poverty have dropped. Other analyses have found that real family incomes increased markedly for blacks, Mexican-Americans, Puerto Ricans, and other Hispanics, American Indians, and whites during the 1960s and increased somewhat for most groups during the 1970s, but declined during the early 1980s.[5] Most observers attribute many of the gains during the 1960s to the sustained economic growth of that period, whereas the lack of progress during the 1970s and 1980s reflects faltering economic growth, rising inflation, and a string of recessions.

This general trend, however, obscures the differences in experience of the population groups represented in the table. The percentages shown for individuals (Panel A) indicate that the poverty rate of whites was about 20 percent higher in 1985 than in 1969. The poverty rate of blacks was basically the same in both years. The Bureau of the Census did not begin to publish statistics on Hispanics until after 1969, so we cannot compare the Hispanic poverty rate in the two years. However, the poverty rate for Hispanics did increase 33 percent between 1979 and 1985. But the poverty rate varies among Hispanic groups: 43 percent of Puerto Ricans, 29 percent of Mexican-Americans, and 22 percent of other Hispanics had incomes below the poverty line in 1985.[6] Because the Current Population Surveys do not include enough American Indians to permit analyses of this group, we do not know the poverty rate for Indians in 1985. The poverty rate for Indians did drop between 1969 and 1979. However, the poverty rate for Indians who lived in traditional Indian areas and on reservations was above the national black poverty rate in 1979.[7]

Panel B shows that the poverty rate for whites in households with female heads changed little between 1969 and 1985, whereas the poverty rate for blacks in such households actually dropped. Although gaps in the data prevent us from comparing poverty rates in 1969 and 1985 for Hispanics and American Indians, our most recent data for each group indicate that the poverty rate among persons living in families with female heads is considerably higher than that for all persons. A recent analysis using a somewhat different income definition of the poor shows that the poverty gap between female-headed families and intact families was considerably higher in 1980 than in 1940.[8] This suggests, as many scholars have noted, that the problems of these persons—both the female heads of household and their children—deserve special attention.

Panel C contains information on children who are related to the householder through blood, marriage, or adoption. In 1985, 99 percent of black and white children under eighteen were in this category. These statistics are perhaps the most depressing of those in Table 4.1, because they indicate that the prevalence of poverty among this group has increased since 1969. Among white children, the poverty rate increased by over 60 percent between 1969 and 1985. The poverty rate did not increase as much for black children, but was nonetheless almost three times the rate for white children in 1985. The poverty rate among Hispanic children increased by over 40 percent between 1979 and 1985. This suggests that children are another population group that deserves special attention in the future fight against poverty.

As Smith points out, the fate of children and female-headed families are interconnected. In 1985, for example, children in female-headed families accounted for 54 percent of poor children but only 20 percent of all children. Among blacks, approximately 50 percent of children lived in female-headed families; over 75 percent of poor black children lived in such families.[9]

As Table 4.1 shows, it is only among the elderly that we see consistent progress throughout the period, as David Hamilton pointed out in Chapter 3. The poverty rate among the white elderly in 1985 was less than half of what it was in 1969, and the poverty rate among the black elderly was less than two-thirds of its 1969 level. A number of researchers have examined these diverse trends in society's treatment of the elderly and children.[10] At least part of the reason has to do with differences in social policy and programs that affect the elderly and those that affect children. For example, Social Security benefits have for some time been indexed to inflation, which protects the elderly against inflation. AFDC benefits (Aid to Families with Dependent Children) and the wages of most young working parents, on the other hand, are not so indexed, and thus many children have not been protected from inflation.

Poverty Rates Adjusted for Noncash Benefits

The figures in the table reflect the amount of cash income available to different population groups; they do not, however, give any indication of the effects of noncash benefits and resources. Those effects are important, since most of the increases in assistance have been in noncash benefits (food stamps, school lunches, public housing, Medicaid, Medicare). For example, in real values, means-tested cash assistance (AFDC, general assistance, Supplemental Security Income, and means-tested veterans' pensions) rose from $17.8 billion in 1965 to $27.6 billion in 1983, an increase of 55 percent. The market value of noncash benefits, on the other hand, rose from $6 billion in 1965 to $106 billion in 1983, an increase of over 1600 percent.[11] Unfortunately, official poverty statistics do not take into account the effects of these noncash benefits.

The Bureau of the Census in the 1980s has begun to produce a series of reports called *Estimates of Poverty Including the Value of Noncash Benefits.* Using the most generous definition of the value of noncash benefits (the market value), one finds that the poverty rate for all persons in 1983 would be reduced from 15.2 to 10.2 percent, a decrease of 33 percent. The poverty rate for children under six goes from 25.0 to 18.2 percent after such adjustment, a decrease of 28 percent, while the poverty rate for the elderly goes from 14.1 to 3.3 percent, a decrease of over 75 percent. This reflects the larger expenditures on Medicare ($56 billion in 1983) than on all other noncash transfer programs combined. Further, the adjusted poverty rate for white persons in 1983 is 8.6 percent, slightly less than the *unadjusted* poverty rate for white persons in 1969. The adjusted poverty rate for black persons in

TABLE 4.2 PERCENTAGE OF INDIVIDUALS BELOW THE POVERTY LINE, BY AREA, 1985

Group	Metro: Central Cities	Metro: Outside Central Cities	Nonmetro	Total
ALL PERSONS				
White	14.9	7.4	15.6	11.4
Black	32.1	21.7	42.6	31.3
Mexican-American	30.7	NA	38.7	28.8
Puerto Rican	49.4	NA	NA	43.3
PERSONS IN HOUSEHOLDS WITH FEMALE HEADS				
White	37.8	20.4	35.5	29.8
Black	53.6	43.3	63.9	53.2
Mexican-American	51.8	NA	61.2	47.3
Puerto Rican	74.7	NA	NA	73.1
RELATED CHILDREN UNDER EIGHTEEN IN FAMILIES				
White	23.6	9.8	19.4	15.6
Black	45.5	31.6	51.4	43.1
Mexican-American	21.1	NA	45.1	37.4
Puerto Rican	16.9	NA	NA	58.6
PERSONS SIXTY-FIVE AND OVER				
White	11.6	7.9	15.1	11.0
Black	27.0	25.7	47.8	31.3
Mexican-American	28.1	NA	NA	23.4
Puerto Rican	NA	NA	NA	39.2

Source: U.S. Bureau of the Census, *Poverty in the United States: 1985,* Table 6, pp. 27–34, and Table 12, pp. 69–71.

1983 is 21.2 percent, considerably lower than their *unadjusted* poverty rate in 1969 (32.2 percent). The greater effect of the in-kind transfer programs for black (and also Hispanic) persons is due to the lower incomes of minority group members, leading to a stronger likelihood of eligibility for noncash transfer programs.

But it should be noted that there is a great deal of controversy involved in measuring the value and impact of noncash transfers on well-being and poverty. My purpose here is not to explore this debate; however, it is important to remember that our policy choices since 1969 have been to put our resources into noncash transfers, which are not reflected in our official statistics. I think we should be disturbed by the official statistics, but we should keep in mind that these statistics do not take the expanded noncash benefits into account.

Poverty Outside the Nation's Central Cities

Although the Kerner Report and much recent work on minority poverty have concentrated on cities, the poverty rate in nonmetropolitan areas remains quite high as well. Table 4.2 contains the percentage of selected population groups that were below the poverty line in 1985 in both metropolitan and nonmetropolitan areas. The poverty rates for all persons in each racial or ethnic group are higher in nonmetropolitan areas than in either central cities or metropolitan areas outside the central city. Among blacks, the percentage below the poverty line is actually about one-third higher in nonmetropolitan areas than in metropolitan areas.

The figures for persons in female-headed families indicate that, among whites, the prevalence of poverty in 1985 was slightly higher in central cities than in nonmetropolitan areas. For both blacks and Mexican-Americans, however, the rates in this category are higher in nonmetropolitan areas than in central cities.

The poverty rate for white children under eighteen living in families in which they are related to the head is higher in central cities than in nonmetropolitan areas. Again, this is not the case for blacks and Mexican-Americans. Over half of black children in nonmetropolitan areas were in families with incomes that placed them below the poverty line.

For both blacks and whites, the poverty rate of persons sixty-five and over was higher in nonmetropolitan areas than in central cities. Almost half of blacks sixty-five and over in metropolitan areas lived in families with incomes below the poverty line.

The point of this comparison is not that the problems of the central cities have been exaggerated or that our attention should be focused on nonmetropolitan areas, but rather that to focus exclusively on central cities is to ignore the rural areas, where poverty is also a serious problem. For American Indians on reservations the poverty rate is extraordinarily high: 44.8 percent of the population in 1980 was below the poverty line.[12] Focusing on what central cities, nonmetropolitan areas, and reservations have in common can perhaps tell us more about the causes of poverty than focusing exclusively on central cities, even though more of the poor live in central cities than in nonmetropolitan areas.

ANTIPOVERTY EFFORTS SINCE KERNER

The Kerner Report made a number of recommendations about how to fight poverty and disadvantage in the central cities of urban areas. Some were implemented; others were not. Since 1968, a number of other analyses of poverty have offered their own suggestions for dealing with these problems.

TABLE 4.3 ALTERNATIVE PROPOSALS FOR DEALING WITH POVERTY IN URBAN AREAS

Kerner Report (1968)	Working Seminar (1987)	Wilson (1987)
A. EMPLOYMENT		
1. Economic growth 2. Public jobs 3. Training 4. Child care 5. Recruit minorities	1. Require people to work	1. Economic growth 2. Increase competitiveness 3. Training 4. Child care 5. Relocation assistance
B. EDUCATION		
1. Eliminate segregation 2. Ensure quality education in ghetto 3. Improved community-school relations 4. Expanded opportunities for higher education	1. Role of families and churches 2. Schools should impose high standards	
C. WELFARE		
1. Uniform national level of assistance 2. Long-term: guaranteed income 3. Child care	1. Work requirements 2. Transitional cash benefits 3. Tax breaks for low-wage earners 4. Allow state and local innovation	1. Standard AFDC benefit adjusted for inflation 2. Child-support assurance program 3. Family allowance 4. Child care
D. HEALTH		
1. Discussion of health problems	1. Cited lack of insurance	

Table 4.3 summarizes the recommendations from three separate analyses of poverty: the Kerner Report, the Working Seminar on Family and American Welfare Policy, and Wilson's *Truly Disadvantaged.* Let us compare these three sets of recommendations and examine the evidence regarding their effectiveness and viability in the areas of employment, education, social-welfare policy, and health. These areas were chosen on the assumption that jobs, human capital, and social-welfare policy are most important in the attempt to fight poverty.

Employment

Both the Kerner Report and Wilson placed a great deal of emphasis on economic growth and the creation of private-sector jobs. To this general recommendation, Wilson adds the idea that the United States needs to increase its competitiveness in the world economy, thereby preventing the loss of jobs to other countries. The fact that most of the gains against poverty were made in the 1960s suggests that economic growth is one of the most important strategies for fighting poverty, if not the most important. Unfortunately, it has also turned out to be one of the most difficult aims to achieve. As one analyst points out, "The frustrations involved in economists' search to find ways of stimulating employment are immense and long-standing. . . . Vigorous booms cannot be created."[13] Another side of this is that recessions are disastrous for the poor and the near-poor.

The Kerner Report called for the creation of public jobs to supplement new and existing jobs in the private sector. The 1970s was a period in which a number of different approaches to creating employment were undertaken. Some programs were designed to combat structural unemployment: unemployment among those who were never employed or who had been displaced by changes in local economies. Others were designed to combat cyclical unemployment: that due to the recessions of the 1970s.

The programs of the mid-1960s and early 1970s (e.g., Job Corps, Neighborhood Youth Corps, and Operation Mainstream) were targeted at minorities, welfare recipients, low-income youth, the elderly, and other hard-to-employ groups. The recession of 1970–71 shifted attention from the long-term employability problems of the disadvantaged to the problems of the cyclically unemployed. Although the original version of the Comprehensive Employment and Training Act (CETA) in 1973 focused on training, the deep recession of 1974–75 produced a new emphasis on public-service employment. The 1978 version of CETA reduced that emphasis, and in 1982 the Job Training Partnership Act (JTPA)—with no funds for public-service employment—replaced CETA.

The evidence of the effectiveness of public-sector employment was summarized by Bassi and Ashenfelter in 1986. It is important to realize that a very small proportion of the disadvantaged participated in employment and training programs, but the individuals who benefited most from participation in CETA (in the training or employment components) were, in fact, the most disadvantaged, with the least amount of previous labor-market experience. Further, women benefited more than men; in fact, participation in CETA did not appear to result in post-program gains in earnings for men at all (apparently due to the fact that the major effect of participation was to increase hours worked rather than to increase the wage earned). Although there appear to be real gains to the disadvantaged from public-sector employment programs, it is important to balance these effects against the possible loss of jobs to nondisadvantaged individuals—a substitution or displacement effect. Bassi and Ashenfelter report that structural employment programs resulted in some substitution, and countercyclical programs resulted in more. They point out that "programs that have high substitution rates (and are, therefore, popular with local governments) are unpopular with unions."[14]

Both the Kerner Report and Wilson called for additional support of training programs for the disadvantaged. Again, the evidence suggests that the training programs of the late 1960s and the 1970s were effective in increasing the post-program earnings of the most disadvantaged participants. Bassi and Ashenfelter conclude: "There is some indication that programs providing intensive (and expensive) investment in each participant, such as the Job Corps and the Supported Work Demonstration, have, at least for some groups of the disadvantaged, more than paid for themselves from a society-wide point of view." Although the program's ineffectiveness for men is discouraging, the empirical evidence supports training targeted at disadvantaged and low-skilled individuals.

Both the Kerner Report and Wilson called for improvements in the availability and quality of child care; the lack of adequate child care was also recognized as a barrier to employment by the more conservative Working Seminar. Unfortunately, few concrete suggestions for improvements have been forthcoming. The general liberal position seems to be that if we were to increase the availability of low-skilled jobs and child care, many people, especially women on AFDC, would be able to escape from poverty and leave the public-assistance rolls. Few have given much thought to how much this combined effort would cost, though one estimate is that it would be roughly twice the cost of the existing AFDC program.[15]

Both the Kerner Report and Wilson were concerned

with low minority access to jobs. They differed in identifying the cause of the low access, which resulted in quite different suggestions about how to improve it. The Kerner Report perceived a great deal of discrimination and racism in the labor market and felt that increased efforts to recruit minorities for public-sector and private-sector positions were needed to overcome these barriers. Wilson, on the other hand, felt that the old barriers due to skin color were no longer the major problem, but that the social and physical isolation of urban blacks needed to be attacked.

Since the Kerner Report, the rules and guidelines of affirmative action have been used in an attempt to increase the employment of minorities and women in jobs and organizations where they have been historically underrepresented. Although affirmative action has been widely attacked from both the right and left, the evidence indicates that it was successful in meeting its limited goal: the employment of minorities and women. Jonathan S. Leonard has carefully examined the evidence on the implementation and outcomes. Both he and the General Accounting Office (GAO) report that affirmative action has been poorly implemented. This has not, however, prevented it from improving the representation of minorities in firms that receive government contracts and in firms that must file reports with the Equal Employment Opportunity Commission (EEOC). Affirmative action has not, on the other hand, led to sustained wage growth among minority-group members.[16]

Wilson has downplayed the importance of affirmative action; he feels that it does not deal with the problems of the most disadvantaged, and that in order to deal with their problems we must develop universal programs that enjoy the support and commitment of a broad constituency. He does state, however, that "this would certainly not mean the abandonment of race-specific policies that embody either the principle of equality of individual rights or that of group rights."[17]

The evidence does indicate that affirmative action has been most beneficial to young, educated minority-group members.[18] Wilson believes that we should emphasize programs that help the poor to obtain jobs in the private sector. This would include both relocation assistance and transitional employment benefits—government assistance to help urban blacks relocate to where jobs were, and to establish themselves there.

There is both a precedent for and evidence about the effectiveness of relocation. From the 1950s through the 1980s, the federal government provided assistance to American Indians to relocate from reservations and depressed rural areas to cities where jobs were more plentiful. A number of cities were selected, and many Indians relocated over the years. These programs were very controversial, not least among Indians themselves, since relocation disrupted the family and community ties on which Indians have traditionally relied. Nonetheless, an analysis sponsored by the Brookings Institution showed that relocation was beneficial to a number of American Indians—that is, they were better off than individuals with similar characteristics who remained on reservations.[19]

Education

Both the Kerner Report and the Working Seminar placed a great deal of emphasis on schools and education as possible solutions to the problems of the poor. Wilson, on the other hand, mentions education only in passing, and makes no specific proposals for improving education and educational opportunities. As one would expect, the Kerner proposals and those of the Working Seminar are quite different. The former suggested that efforts be made to eliminate segregation, ensure quality education in the inner city, improve community-school relations, and expand opportunities for higher education; the Working Seminar suggested that families and churches should be more involved in the socialization and education of children and that schools should impose high standards on all students.

There is still controversy over whether school desegregation benefits black children. According to Nathan Glazer, the educational benefits for black children are quite small, but Christopher Jencks argues that most studies focus on the first year of desegregation, and that studies that look beyond the first year find educational benefits at least as large as those from Head Start and Title I.[20]

The evidence regarding efforts to improve education for minority and disadvantaged children is also conflicting. Glazer argues that research results indicate that preschool and elementary programs are more effective than high-school programs, justifying an emphasis on the former. Jencks finds the evidence unconvincing: "All in all, the cumulative record of twenty years of research on these issues is not terribly impressive, primarily because federal agencies have seldom sponsored the kinds of long-term studies we would need to answer such questions."[21]

Both the Kerner Report and the Working Seminar emphasized the importance of community involvement in the schools. We know even less about the effects of community involvement on test scores than we know about the effects of desegregation and compensatory educational programs. We do know that one effect of bilingual Hispanic educational programs and special educational programs for Indian students has been to increase the involvement of Hispanic and Indian parents in the public schools.[22] Most observers assume that this will lead to improvements in the educational achievement of the children.

The Working Seminar also emphasized the importance of high standards in the public schools. Some argue that the successful schools are those with "strong" principals and good community-school relations.[22] The evidence on the success of such schools is largely anecdotal, however, and we have no firm empirical evidence that high standards alone can improve educational performance.

The Kerner Report put a good deal of emphasis on higher education, and during the late 1960s and early 1970s a great deal of emphasis was placed on expanding higher educational opportunities. Neither the Working Seminar nor Wilson have devoted systematic attention to this issue. Both seem to see higher education as beyond the grasp of the most disadvantaged, and thus not a potential solution to their problems. The political climate since the late 1970s has prompted cutbacks in scholarships and financial aid, which appears to have had a deleterious effect on the college enrollments of disadvantaged youngsters.[24]

Social-Welfare Policy

Although the underlying aim of all three sets of proposals reviewed here was to reduce the need for welfare through increasing the human capital and job opportunities for disadvantaged individuals, each set also contained some recommendations about the social-welfare system. The Kerner Report recommended that a uniform national level of assistance be established, and that this assistance be financed completely at the federal level. This temporary measure was to be followed by the implementation of a guaranteed income or negative income tax.[25] Wilson made a similar suggestion, although his proposal was narrower: establishing a national standard AFDC benefit that would be adjusted yearly for inflation. In addition, Wilson advocated a national Child Support Assurance Program, through which the absent parents of children would be required to pay child support, with government supplementation if necessary.[26] He also advocated a family allowance like those in some Western European countries.

The welfare-reform proposals of the Working Seminar take a different tack. Their major emphasis was on work requirements and sanctions: all individuals who receive welfare and who are able to work should be required to do so; those who refuse should be punished by withholding benefits. Cash assistance should be viewed as "transitional" in most cases—i.e., every effort should be made to get people off this assistance.

The Working Seminar also differed in its views of federal versus local control of welfare policy. Although it saw some utility in federally set benefit levels, it preferred to allow states and local governments to experiment and innovate with programs and benefit levels.

Finally, the Working Seminar argued that low-income workers should be treated better by the tax system than at present—a view shared by many other analysts.[27] In sum, the Working Seminar felt that work should be required and rewarded and that failure to work should be sanctioned.

Such proposals to reform social-welfare policy strike a responsive chord in most Americans, who see the current system as inefficient and ineffective, if not downright harmful. Few scholars have seriously tried to determine which aspects of the current system are worth retaining, which should be modified, and which should be completely discarded. Some who have done so argue that "the income support strategy of the past two decades has worked. Providing cash and in-kind transfers has reduced the extent of both poverty and income disparities across age and racial groups."[28]

In regard to state and local experimentation, others conclude that

> *we have been engaged in an experiment over the past ten years. This experiment has been carried out at the expense of single mothers, and its results can be judged a failure. We have cut back AFDC benefits considerably. There has been no noticeable effect on family structure or work. We can be sure, however, that its impact on the well-being of single mothers was noticed by the families. We have also conducted an experiment in allowing benefits to vary [between] states for years. Here, too, there is little evidence that these differences had any noticeable effect on work or family structure.*[29]

These authors also find no evidence that government transfer policies are responsible for the low rates of labor-force participation by black youth.

Health

The Kerner Report pointed out the poor health conditions in the central cities, but made no specific recommendations for dealing with them. The Working Seminar saw the lack of health insurance among low-wage earners as a problem, but offered no cure. Herbert Nickens recently summarized some of the major health problems facing minority-group members in the United States. First, black mortality rates are substantially worse than those of whites; Hispanic and Native American rates fall somewhere between. Second, minorities are less likely than whites to have health insurance and more likely to have other problems in gaining access to health care. Some of the access problems faced by minorities are also faced by low-income whites.[30]

Paul Starr argues that insurance coverage should be provided to everyone, and that the costs of doing so are not prohibitive. He also argues that one of the programs developed in the late 1960s, community health centers, offers a good approach for improving access among the urban poor. There is evidence that these centers provided better health care at lower costs to those in the central city than did other arrangements. Clinics operated by the Indian Health Service or individual tribes on Indian reservations have also had a good record of improving health-care delivery.[31] Consequently, it seems clear that a combination of health insurance and community health centers would be a good way to improve the health of minority-group members and low-income whites.

SUMMARY AND CONCLUSIONS

The Kerner Report, the Working Seminar, and Wilson have concentrated on urban areas. The reasons for this are clear in the case of the Kerner Report, since its charge was to examine conditions in cities. The Working Seminar and Wilson, though they have quite different ideological orienta-

TABLE 4.4 THE CONCENTRATION OF POVERTY, 1985

Group	Percentage of the Poor in Central Cities	Percentage of the Poor in Non-metro-politan Areas	Percentage of the Poor in Central-City Poverty Areas[a]	Percentage of the Poor in Non-metro-politan Poverty Areas[a]
Whites	35.5	32.6	14.2[b]	9.7[b]
Blacks	60.9	22.5	47.4[b]	14.5[b]
Mexican-Americans	54.8	15.1	31.3	7.1
Puerto Rican	89.0	NA	75.5	NA
Total population[c]	42.9	29.6	23.8[b]	11.2[b]

Note: With the exceptions indicated by note b, these figures are based on individuals and are computed from information in Tables 6 and 12 in U.S. Bureau of the Census, *Poverty in the United States: 1985.*

[a]Poverty areas are defined in terms of census tracts (in metropolitan areas) or minor civil divisions (townships, districts, etc., in nonmetropolitan areas) in which 20% or more of the population was below the poverty level in 1979, based on the 1980 census.

[b]These figures are based on families and are computed using information from Table 16, pp. 78–88, in *Poverty in the United States: 1985.* All other figures are based on individuals and are computed from information in Tables 6 and 12 in U.S. Bureau of the Census, *Poverty in the United States: 1985.*

[c]In 1985, 29.6% of the nonpoor lived in central cities and 21.5% of the nonpoor lived in nonmetropolitan areas. So 51.2% of the nonpoor, but only 27.5% of the poor, lived in metropolitan areas outside central cities.

tions, share an underlying assumption that problems are more serious in cities than elsewhere. The Working Seminar goes so far as to say that "poor white children in rural areas are probably not suffering under the harsh conditions most poor black children meet in urban areas." This may or may not be true, but it is worth careful investigation. It is not enough for people on different sides of this issue to quote anecdotes to one another, for it is too easy to find examples of harsh conditions anywhere. It is my position that continuing to focus on urban minority poverty may lead us to wrong conclusions. First, however, let me demonstrate why it is so tempting to focus on the central cities as the seat of all problems.

Table 4.4 contains information on the residential concentration of poverty among different minority groups (except American Indians in 1985, since the census studies do not provide adequate information on this group). A little over one-third of the white poor live in central cities, a little less than one-third live in nonmetropolitan areas, and a similar proportion in metropolitan areas outside the central city. Only a very small percentage of the white poor are concentrated in poverty areas, in either the central city or nonmetropolitan areas. This is not the situation for minority groups: Over 60 percent of the black poor live in central cities, and almost 50 percent live in central-city poverty areas. Over 50 percent of the poor of Mexican descent live in central cities, and almost one-third live in central-city poverty areas. Three-fourths of the Puerto Rican poor live in central-city poverty areas. Consequently, it is very tempting to focus on inner cities as the major problem area. However, the figures in the bottom row of Table 4.4 indicate that by doing so we are examining less than one-fourth of the total poor population; three-fourths of the poor in the United States live outside central-city poverty areas. Further, Chapter 5, by Adams, Duncan, and Rodgers, shows that a majority of the people who are poor for extended periods of time live outside the most highly concentrated poverty areas.

More important, a focus on the causes of poverty among

TABLE 4.5 POPULATION AND LABOR-MARKET CHARACTERISTICS OF PERSONS IN VARIOUS GEOGRAPHICAL AREAS, 1980

Area	Median Age	Families with Female Heads (%)	Population 16 and Over in the Labor Force (%)	Labor Force 16 and Over Unemployed (%)
WHITES				
Central cities	31.8	14.7	62.0	5.7
Metro[a]	31.0	10.0	64.5	5.4
Nonmetropolitan	31.2	9.0	58.2	6.7
BLACKS				
Central cities	25.4	41.6	59.2	12.8
Metro[a]	24.6	30.2	64.9	9.6
Nonmetropolitan	23.9	31.8	53.2	11.6
AMERICAN INDIANS				
Central cities	24.9	28.9	62.9	12.3
Metro[a]	24.8	18.6	64.0	11.0
Nonmetropolitan	21.5	22.4	52.7	15.3
HISPANICS				
Central cities	23.5	24.3	62.3	9.3
Metro[a]	23.2	14.5	66.5	8.3
Nonmetropolitan	21.9	14.1	58.5	9.7

Source: U.S. Bureau of the Census, *Census of the Population, 1980: General Social and Economic Characteristics,* Tables 140, 141, 143, 144, 149, 150, 151, 153, 154, and 159.

[a]Metro, outside central cities.

the central-city population may lead us to conclude that unique features of these areas are the source of the problem. Before reaching this conclusion, we need to ask ourselves whether there are common features of disadvantaged central-city and nonmetropolitan areas that account for poverty. That is, it could be that while more poor people live in central cities, the basic causes of poverty are similar in both geographical areas.[32]

Table 4.5 allows us to compare key characteristics of the populations in central cities, metropolitan areas outside the central cities, and nonmetropolitan areas. The advantage of using the 1980 census information here is that it allows us to look at American Indians as well as whites, blacks, and Hispanics. Factors that are often mentioned as unique to central cities are a very young population, a high prevalence of female-headed families, low rates of labor-force participation, and high rates of unemployment. The Table shows that for each racial or ethnic group, the median age of the population is actually lower in nonmetropolitan areas than in central cities. The prevalence of female-headed families is higher in central cities for each group, but the percentage of the population sixteen and over that is in the labor force is higher in central cities than in nonmetropolitan areas. For blacks, the unemployment rate was slightly higher in central cities than in nonmetropolitan areas, but for the other groups, the unemployment rate was slightly—and in the case of American Indians considerably—higher in nonmetropolitan areas than in central cities. Consequently, the population characteristics, labor-market characteristics, and poverty rates of both places suggest that we should determine whether the causes of poverty are similar. This could lead us to even more universal solutions and programs to deal with poverty than those envisioned by Wilson. The question deserves more attention than it is receiving in current research and policy discussions.

The evidence regarding current and proposed policies suggests some modest and cautious conclusions. First, some policies that are currently under attack deserve to be defended. These include AFDC, affirmative action, and school desegregation. I agree with Ellwood and Summers that we have experimented with low and state-varying AFDC benefits long enough, and heartily support their recommendation—as well as those of Wilson, Danziger, and others—that a national standard AFDC benefit level needs to be set, and that this benefit should be adjusted for inflation each year. Affirmative action seems to have been successful in meeting its limited goals and deserves to be retained as a means of improving minority access to employment opportunities; its major failure appears to be that it has not been implemented forcefully enough. The evidence also indicates that school desegregation is an effective way to improve the educational opportunities of minority children. In Chapter 7, Gary Orfield suggests that persisting racial segregation has led to the concentration of black and Hispanic youngsters in schools with limited resources and poor educational environments. Desegregation should lead to improvements in the schools attended by minority students.

Research suggests that we also reconsider policies that have fallen into political disfavor. These include community health centers, training programs for disadvantaged workers, and public-sector employment programs. If these programs are developed in ways that make it clear they are directed at *all* disadvantaged individuals, white and nonwhite, and in both metropolitan and nonmetropolitan areas, they may become politically viable once more.

Finally, our experience with past innovations indicates that we should carefully evaluate new ideas before proceeding with large-scale implementation. Workfare programs that require individuals to work or participate in training have become popular—they provide training opportunities, which pleases liberals, but also enforce work requirements, which pleases conservatives. We are now accumulating evidence on the kinds of workfare programs that are most effective. Programs to expand health-insurance coverage are in the experimental stage in Wisconsin and elsewhere, and we will gradually accumulate evidence on their costs and effectiveness. Workfare and health-insurance programs may also become tools in the fight against poverty, but we should proceed cautiously with their evaluation and implementation.

Part III

A GROWING URBAN UNDERCLASS

"Segregation and poverty have created in the racial ghetto a destructive environment totally unknown to most white Americans," the Kerner Report stated.

"What white Americans," the report continued, "have never fully understood—but what the Negro can never forget—is that white society is deeply implicated in the ghetto. White institutions created it, white institutions maintain it, and white society condones it."

The urban ghetto—and its destructive environment—is still with us twenty years later, and it is growing. In 1968 the Kerner Report said that the urban ghetto resulted from a mixture of both racial and economic causes. The same is true today, though some disagree as to the relative strength of those two factors.

Increasingly today intractable urban problems are spoken of in terms of an urban "underclass." Some find this classification offensive and unjustifiable—and it is when it is used, as some conservatives do, to make a "culture" of bad behaviors the cause of poverty for the people involved, to "blame the victim." In fact, these behaviors—welfare dependency, chronic unemployment, and single-parent families, for example—are not the causes but rather the *symptoms,* the results of what William Julius Wilson and his colleagues in Chapter 7 call a legacy of both "historic racial oppression and of continued class subordination in the United States."

In Chapter 5, Adams, Duncan, and Rodgers concentrate on the *persistence* of urban poverty rather than on the concept of an underclass—how long urban poverty lasts and how hard it is to escape. They show that in the nation's central cities poverty has become more prevalent since the Kerner Report, it is deeper, and it is more persistent and harder to escape. Nearly half of these persistently poor are children.

In Chapter 6, Gary Orfield focuses on racial segregation. He finds that schools for blacks and Hispanics are resegregating and that housing in America's cities, especially for blacks, is still starkly segregated. He makes the point that this segregation has terrible negative consequences for the people who are so isolated.

In Chapter 7, Wilson, Aponte, Kirschenman, and Wacquant detail the existence of a large, growing, and spreading urban underclass in America's central cities—highly concentrated and principally black and Hispanic. This underclass, they show, has resulted from joblessness in the central city, the exodus of working families, and the deterioration of inner-city social organization. The underclass suffers from a "concentration effect" of severe restrictions and restraints on opportunities that go with living in neighborhoods of concentrated disadvantage.

The authors of all the chapters in Part III, though differing somewhat in their approaches, agree that twenty years after the Kerner Report there is a continuing and great contrast between the races in America, especially in the inner cities—in jobs, pay, housing, schools, and opportunities—and that this is not good for America.

CHAPTER 5

The Persistence of Urban Poverty

TERRY K. ADAMS,
GREG J. DUNCAN, AND
WILLARD L. RODGERS

TWENTY YEARS AFTER the urban riots of the 1960s, the issue of urban poverty is again high on the nation's social agenda.

Largely as a result of a *New Yorker* series by Ken Auletta, the public is concerned about a highly visible and apparently growing urban "underclass."[1] Auletta defines the underclass not by income level, but by deviant *behavior*—welfare dependency, failure to complete high school, drug use, criminal activity—and thus revives many of the themes raised in the poverty debates of the 1960s.[2]

Data from the 1980 census has been analyzed to document a second important aspect of urban poverty—its increased geographic *concentration.* For example, in the nation's fifty largest cities, 16 percent of the poor in 1970 lived in poverty areas (census tracts where at least 40 percent of the population was poor); in 1980, 24 percent did.[3] Some commentators argue that the resulting social isolation of the poor is the key feature of urban poverty.[4]

Poverty has yet a third dimension—*persistence.* What makes the problem of urban poverty seem desperate is its apparent persistence—the likelihood that one will never find a decent job or marriage partner, that one's children will share the same fate. Indeed, the very use of the term *underclass* implies that poverty is permanent, that certain characteristic attitudes and behavior will be passed from generation to generation.

Yet, though suitable data have been available, no empirical studies have hitherto focused on the persistence of urban poverty. Our purpose here is to estimate the extent of persistent urban poverty, describe its demographic and behavioral characteristics, and assess whether it has become more or less persistent since the Kerner Report was written.

There are many reasons to view persistence as a crucial dimension of urban poverty. *Income* is probably the most widely used gauge of a household's standard of living and its command over resources. But by itself, a year's income is a flawed measure; a given household may have a temporarily low income (owing, say, to a bad year for a self-employed person or to a brief spell of unemployment), but otherwise be obviously well off. Long-term assessments of household income are more likely to identify households with persistently low standards of living.

Furthermore, a growing body of research suggests that persistent family poverty is related to less schooling and less-successful careers for children.[5] One recent study found that, even when other measures of the economic and demographic status of the family were equal, parental poverty had a variety of detrimental effects on the schooling and early career attainment of children.[6]

IMPORTANT ISSUES

We have tried to delineate a set of useful facts about persistent urban poverty, in order to lend perspective to the more qualitative accounts of it. We have been guided by the following questions from the current debate:

- *How persistent is urban poverty?* Several studies have found that many experiences of poverty are short. Without examining geographic differences, Bane and Ellwood estimate that about three-fifths of all poverty spells end within three years, and only one-seventh of them last as long as eight years.[7] However, people with longer spells of poverty will obviously show up as poor in more years; at any given time, more than half the poor are in the midst of spells lasting at least eight years. Nonetheless, at least some of those identified as urban poor in single-year census data are poor only temporarily. Thus it is important to compare the characteristics of *all* the urban poor in a single year with those of the persistently poor, in order to gauge how useful single-year poverty data are for making inferences about *persistent* poverty.

- *Has urban poverty become more persistent?* Several changes—in the nation's urban industries, in the geographic concentration of poverty, in the number of one-parent families, and in the perceived growth of an underclass—all suggest that urban poverty has become more persistent since the 1960s. Census Bureau figures show that poverty rates for the nation's central cities rose by half (from 12.7 to 19.0 percent) between 1969 and 1985. But these single-year poverty figures do not demonstrate an increased *persistence* of poverty; that can be done only with multi-year data from the same set of families.

Are the persistently poor an urban "underclass"? Auletta defines the underclass solely in terms of deviant behavior, but he reckons its size solely in terms of income.[8] It may be that certain behavioral indicators of underclass membership (welfare receipt, female headship, little schooling) are correlated with low income, but we also know that a substantial number of intact working families, the elderly, and the disabled are in danger of being persistently poor. Ricketts and Sawhill found only a rather modest overlap between neighborhoods with high rates of poverty-level *income* and those with high rates of underclass *behavior.*[9] We will examine the strength of this correlation between poverty and underclass behavior.

How concentrated is persistent poverty? The striking growth in the concentration of the urban poor raises questions about the geographic concentration of the persistently poor. More specifically, how much are the disadvantages of persistent family poverty compounded by the problems of living in poor neighborhoods?

Is poverty different from city to city? Cities are tremendously diverse in population, economy, and politics. Only a handful of cities account for the bulk of the country's increased geo-

FIGURE 5.1 URBAN POVERTY, 1974–83

1980 Census figures show that one in every seven individuals (13.4%) living in urban areas was poor in 1979. We estimate that over the decade between 1974 and 1983, over one-third of the urban population was poor at least once but only one in twenty (5.2%) was poor at least 80 percent of the time. Among blacks three in five (60.0%) were poor at least once and one in five (21.1%) was poor at least 80 percent of the time.

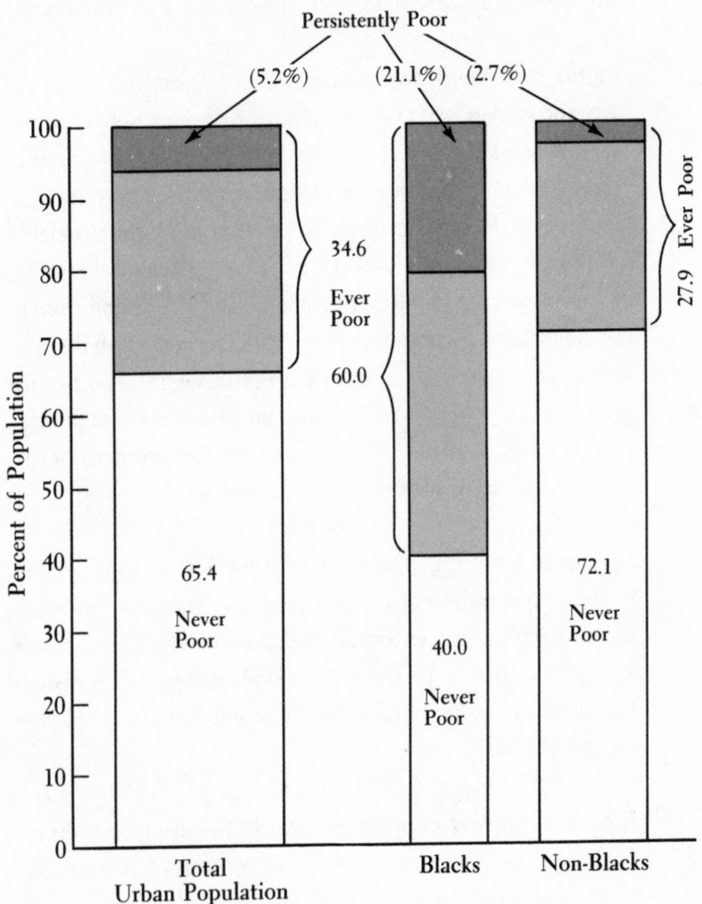

graphical concentration of poverty between 1970 and 1980; a number of cities actually decreased in concentration.[10] An examination of persistent urban poverty clearly must consider differences from city to city.

Our analysis is based on data from the Survey Research Center's Panel Study of Income Dynamics (PSID), which has conducted annual interviews with a nationally representative sample of about five thousand families since 1968; we restricted the sample to individuals living in the fifty-six most highly urbanized counties of the country.[11] We wanted to tie estimates of persistent poverty to 1980 census information on single-year poverty, so we selected a ten-year span of income information (1974–83) that roughly brackets the year (1979) for which income and poverty status are measured in the 1980 census.[12] We define poverty as *persistent* if household income was below the official poverty level in at least eight of the ten years.

A PROFILE OF PERSISTENT POVERTY

Is poverty permanent? The 1980 census shows that, in large urban areas, about one person in every seven (13.4 percent) was poor in 1979.[13] If poverty were a permanent state, the same individuals, and therefore the same percentage of the urban population, would be poor for the entire ten years of this study, 1974–83. If the opposite were true—if very few of those who were poor in one year were also poor in any other—then virtually everyone would be poor in one year or two out of ten.

The truth lies between the extremes (Figure 5.1)—there

TABLE 5.1 CHARACTERISTICS OF THE URBAN POOR

	Persistently Poor (8 or More Years, 1974–83)	Poor in 1979	Total U.S. Urban Population
CHARACTERISTICS OF INDIVIDUAL			
AGE AND ETHNICITY			
Black, 0–17 years	32%	19%	7%
White, 0–17	13	16	19
Black, 18–64	28	25	12
White, 18–64	13	27	52
All races, 65 and older	13	13	10
ETHNICITY OF INDIVIDUAL			
Black	66%	51%	21%
White	34	49	79
CHARACTERISTICS OF INDIVIDUAL'S HOUSEHOLD			
ETHNICITY, SEX, AND MARITAL STATUS OF HOUSEHOLD HEAD			
Black male	21%	18%	12%
Black female, never married	13	8	2
Black female, previously married	33	26	6
White male	12	24	64
White female	22	25	16
SCHOOLING OF HOUSEHOLD HEAD			
0–8 grades	49%	29%	12%
9–11	29	27	17
12	18	32	33
13 or more	4	11	38
AGE OF HOUSEHOLD HEAD			
Under 25 years	11%	13%	7%
25–34	14	25	27
35–44	24	21	20
45–54	17	15	21
55–64	13	11	12
65 and older	21	16	12

TABLE 5.1 *(Continued)*

	Persistently Poor (8 or More Years, 1974–83)	Poor in 1979	Total U.S. Urban Population
CHILDREN IN HOUSEHOLD?			
Yes, some under age 6	41%	32%	2%
Yes, none under age 6	34	31	32
No children	25	37	43
SIZE OF HOUSEHOLD			
1 person	17%	21%	14%
2–4	34	48	62
5 or more	49	31	24
Estimated fraction of U.S. urban population	5.2%	13.4%	100.0%
Number of observations	868	1585	5499

Source: Panel Study of Income Dynamics.

is substantial, but by no means complete, turnover. About one-third (34.6 percent) of the urban population lived below the poverty line at least one year, but only one-twentieth (5.2 percent) were poor at least 80 percent of the time. For blacks, the proportions were higher than for the urban population as a whole—three in five blacks were poor at least once, and one in five was poor at least 80 percent of the time.[14] Persistent poverty is more than seven times as prevalent among urban blacks as among the rest of the urban population.

Who, then, are the urban persistently poor? The demographic characteristics of three classes of urban individuals (and of the heads of their households) are compared in Table 5.1—the persistently poor, those who were poor in 1979, and the whole urban population.

As an example, let us see how black children 17 and younger fare: they are 7 percent of the entire urban population, but are overrepresented among the 1979 poor (19 percent) and particularly overrepresented among the persistently poor (32 percent). Clearly, persistent poverty in urban areas is considerably more concentrated among black children than the one-year poverty figures would indicate.

The urban persistently poor differ demographically from the other groups, including those poor in a single year. Persistent poverty in the cities is heavily concentrated among blacks, and among people living in households whose head was a woman or someone who did not complete high school. Half (51 percent) of the urban poor in 1979 were black, but of the urban persistently poor, two-thirds (66 percent) were black. In these large urban counties, one-third (34 percent) of the 1979 poor lived in households headed by black women; of the persistently poor, nearly half (46 percent) did.

The media image of urban poverty often shows a young, never-married black woman as household head. We found, though, that this image does not fit even a substantial minority of the urban persistently poor. Only one in eight of them lived in a household headed by a never-married black woman, and only one in four lived in households in which the head—male or female, black or white—was younger than thirty-five. Indeed, the age distribution of the heads of households among the persistently poor is about the same as that among the entire urban population. The age group most overrepresented is the elderly, who have the least favorable employment and marriage options.

Education—or lack of it—counts for much more. In the large urban counties, nearly four-fifths (78 percent) of the persistently poor lived in households where the head had not graduated from high school. The proportion is much lower both among the one-year poor (56 percent) and among the entire urban population (29 percent).

ARE THE PERSISTENTLY POOR A BEHAVIORAL "UNDERCLASS," OR ARE THEY "DESERVING"?

Much discussion of the urban "underclass" defines it in terms of status and behavior—welfare dependency, broken families, unemployment, incomplete schooling, drug use, and so forth. Our PSID data provide information on the first four of these.

The first category is welfare dependency, which we defined as reliance on funds from two major income-tested programs—Aid to Families with Dependent Children (AFDC) and Supplemental Security Income (SSI)—for more than half of the family income in 1979. Roughly half of the urban persistently poor (49 percent) were welfare-dependent in this sense. Even more of them had other "underclass" characteristics—they were living in a household where the head was female (68 percent), were not employed at the time of the 1980 interview (74 percent), or had not completed high school (78 percent). Virtually all of the urban persistently poor (93 percent) showed at least one "underclass" trait—but so did nearly half of the entire urban population (49 percent). About one-third of the persistently poor (31 percent) had all four traits—significantly more than the 1979 poor (17 percent) or the entire urban population (3 percent).

So some "underclass" traits are visible among the persis-

TABLE 5.2 DISTRIBUTION OF URBAN POPULATION, 1979 POOR, AND PERSISTENTLY POOR

	PSID Estimates, Based on ZIP Code						Census Estimates (Bane and Jargowsky, 1987), Based on Census Tract	
	BLACK			WHITE AND OTHER			BLACK	NON-HISPANIC WHITE
FRACTION OF PERSONS IN 1980 ZIP CODE OF RESIDENCE WHO WERE POOR	PERSISTENTLY POOR (8 OR MORE YEARS, (1974–83)	POOR IN 1979	TOTAL U.S. URBAN POPULATION	PERSISTENTLY POOR (8 OR MORE YEARS, 1974–83)	POOR IN 1979	TOTAL U.S. URBAN POPULATION	POOR IN 1979	POOR IN 1979
20 percent or more	77%	74%	66%	61%	27%	10%	84%	34%
30 percent or more	49%	41%	32%	16%	11%	2%	63%	15%
40 percent or more	8%	8%	8%	3%	1%	0%	36%	6%
Unweighted number of observations	793	1367	3289	75	218	2210		
Weighted percent of total urban population	3%	7%	21%	2%	7%	79%		

tently poor. But so are many traits often used to characterize the "deserving" poor—living in a household whose head was either elderly (21 percent), seriously disabled (33 percent), living with a spouse (24 percent), or working a substantial amount (22 percent).[15] Between one-fifth and one-third of the persistently poor had each of these characteristics; a clear majority (61 percent) had one or more of them. Clearly, there are data to support either stereotype—underclass or deserving poor.

THE GEOGRAPHY OF URBAN POVERTY

Are the persistently poor more highly concentrated in high-poverty areas than other urban residents are? Yes—especially if they're black. Take the middle category of concentration shown in Table 5.2—ZIP Code areas where at least 30 percent of the population is poor.[16] About 16 percent of persistently poor urban whites live in such areas, while 49 percent of persistently poor urban blacks do; in other words, they are three times as likely as whites to live there. Among the one-year poor, only about 11 percent of whites live in such areas; 41 percent of blacks do.

Most striking, though, is the fact that a majority of the persistently poor, even of persistently poor blacks, do *not* live in areas of highly concentrated poverty. Thus a focus on "high-poverty" areas—in most of which, it should be remembered, the majority of persons are *not* poor—misses most of the persistently poor.

It should also be noted that *nonpoor* urban blacks seem

TABLE 5.3 ONE-YEAR POVERTY AND PERSISTENT POVERTY AMONG INDIVIDUALS IN MAJOR U.S. CITIES

	1980 Total Population (Census Figures)		1980 Population who were Poor in 1979 (Census Figures)		1980 Population who were Persistently Poor 1974–83 (Estimated from PSID)	
CITY	RANK	NUMBER	NUMBER	% OF TOTAL POPULATION	ESTIMATED NUMBER	% OF TOTAL POPULATION
New York, N.Y.	1	6,963,692	1,391,981	20.0	678,595	9.7
Chicago, Ill.	2	2,965,631	601,410	20.3	324,311	10.9
Los Angeles, Calif.	3	2,907,573	477,976	16.4	249,080	8.6
Philadelphia, Pa.	4	1,653,164	340,517	20.6	178,748	10.8
Houston, Tex.	5	1,578,339	199,755	12.7	108,584	6.9
Detroit, Mich.	6	1,182,733	258,575	21.9	147,234	12.4
Dallas, Tex.	7	890,062	126,193	14.2	70,071	7.9
San Diego, Calif.	8	811,871	101,034	12.4	45,249	5.6
Phoenix, Ariz.	9	780,111	86,659	11.1	20,663	2.6
Baltimore, Md.	10	769,283	176,476	22.9	97,688	12.7
San Antonio, Tex.	11	770,288	161,288	20.9	87,989	11.4
Indianapolis, Ind.	12	687,739	79,166	11.5	22,934	3.3
San Francisco, Calif.	13	665,032	91,195	13.7	32,120	4.8
Memphis, Tenn.	14	634,672	138,670	21.8	96,763	15.2

	1980 Total Population (Census Figures)		1980 Population who were Poor in 1979 (Census Figures)		1980 Population who were Persistently Poor 1974–83 (Estimated from PSID)	
CITY	RANK	NUMBER	NUMBER	% OF TOTAL POPULATION	ESTIMATED NUMBER	% OF TOTAL POPULATION
Washington, D.C.	15	610,454	113,356	18.6	52,780	8.6
Milwaukee, Wisc.	16	620,154	85,328	13.8	51,476	8.3
San Jose, Calif.	17	619,018	50,569	8.2	11,702	1.9
Cleveland, Ohio	18	564,407	124,860	22.1	81,188	14.4
Columbus, Ohio	19	541,659	89,218	16.5	44,925	8.3
Boston, Mass.	20	529,726	106,770	20.6	49,585	9.4
New Orleans, La.	21	544,539	143,793	26.4	99,952	18.4
Jacksonville, Fla.	22	529,638	84,648	16.0	26,376	5.0
Seattle, Wash.	23	474,153	52,995	11.2	12,341	2.6
Denver, Colo.	24	480,573	65,829	13.7	30,761	6.4
Nashville, Tenn.	25	435,080	55,029	12.6	16,401	3.8
St. Louis, Mo.	26	444,308	96,849	21.8	53,461	12.0
Kansas City, Mo.	27	440,001	57,965	13.2	17,402	4.0
El Paso, Tex.	28	420,102	89,250	21.2	26,955	6.4
Atlanta, Ga.	29	409,424	112,622	27.5	78,347	19.1

to be nearly as likely as persistently poor urban blacks to live in areas with high concentrations of poverty, whether the concentration is 20, 30, or 40 percent.[17] This is not true for whites—which confirms the great importance of race, rather than income, in the residential segregation of blacks.

CITY ESTIMATES

How many persistently poor people are there in various U.S. cities? How large a portion of the population are they?

We found widespread variation in the estimated fraction of a city's population that is persistently poor, ranging from around 2 percent for Seattle and San José, to 19 percent for Atlanta (see Table 5.3).[18] But these cities are also most extreme in their fractions of one-year poor as well; the rankings of the various cities are similar in the two types of poverty. Differences are due to the fact that some cities have a greater proportion of black households and female-headed households—two key factors in our estimated relationship between one-year and persistent poverty.

HAS URBAN POVERTY GROWN MORE PERSISTENT?

In urban areas in 1974–83, about 5 percent of the total population—and 40 percent of the poor—could be characterized as persistently poor. How do these numbers compare

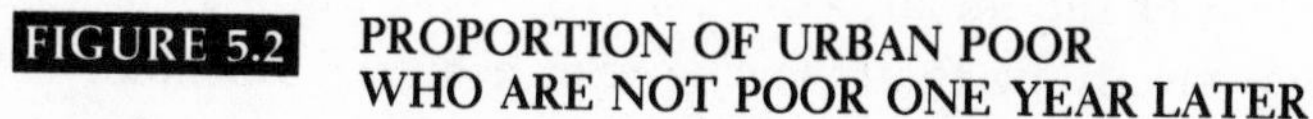

FIGURE 5.2 PROPORTION OF URBAN POOR WHO ARE NOT POOR ONE YEAR LATER

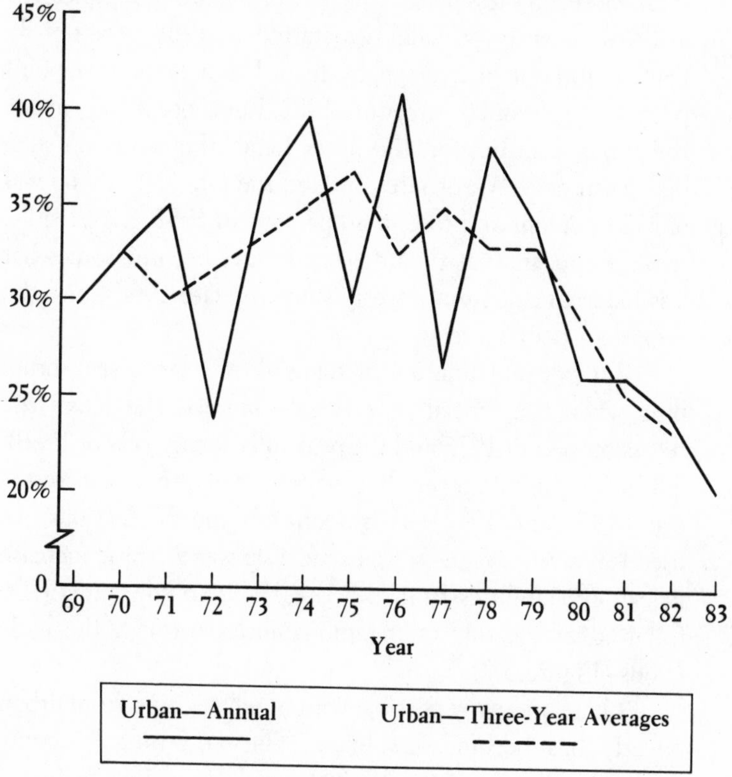

with those of the late 1960s? We know from Census Bureau data that single-year poverty grew in urban areas between the late 1960s and the mid-1980s, but single-year figures do not show whether persistent urban poverty rose comparably.

To gauge persistence, here, we have calculated the proportion of the urban poor in a given year who have exited from poverty by the following year; a higher probability of escape indicates less persistence.[19] For the urban samples, the exit-from-poverty probabilities started in 1968 at about 30 percent and fell, on average, by about half a percentage point per year, to about 20 percent in 1982. For those living outside the urban counties, on the other hand, there was no such decline in poverty-exit rates; in fact, the rate in 1968–69 was only 23 percent and rose to 30 percent in 1982–83. Broadly, then, it appears that the urban poor have become somewhat less likely to exit from poverty since the late 1960s, and the nonurban poor more so.

But exit probabilities fluctuated from year to year, dropping when the official poverty rate jumped the most (the recession year of 1975 and the peak inflationary year of 1980), but moving in rather puzzling ways in some other years (especially 1972 and 1977). To smooth out the fluctuations, we used three-year averages; we found a slow and erratic increase in exit probabilities from the late 1960s to the mid-1970s, followed by steadily falling probabilities through the early 1980s (Figure 5.2).

There are many possible reasons why exiting from urban poverty has become less likely. The worsening economy doubtless played a role, although we were unable to find a precise relationship between changing exit probabilities and shifting national economic conditions. Instead we focused on two related hypotheses: that the changing composition of the poor population made exit more difficult; and that greater economic inequality has made poverty so deep that exit has become more elusive.[20]

We found that demographic factors—the age of the individual; the completed schooling, race, and sex of the household head; and the size of the family—were all very powerful predictors of the likelihood that a poor individual (in either the urban or the nonurban sample) would exit from poverty. Probabilities were lowest for those in households headed by black women and by people with less than a tenth-grade education, for those in very large households, and for the elderly. Probabilities were higher, though still below average, for children and those in families headed by white women.

Quite surprisingly, we found that if the demographic composition of the poor population had remained stable over the period (1970–82), the exit rate would have fallen even more than it did—since, on balance, demographic changes actually enhanced the prospects of exiting from poverty. The proportion of urban poor living in families headed by women did indeed increase sharply over the period, but that negative shift was more than offset by others—particularly the substantial decrease in the proportions living either in very large households or in households headed by someone with less than a high-school education.

We then considered the role of economic status in each of the two years before the possible transition out of poverty—and found them to be even more powerful in predicting whether an individual climbed out of poverty.

It is hardly surprising, of course, that individuals far below the poverty line have the most difficulty climbing out. What is more interesting, however, is that if we adjust for prior economic status, the apparent decline in escape probabilities from the late 1960s to early 1980s is reduced. The poverty of the urban poor has *deepened* considerably—a typical urban poor person in the early 1980s was further below our poverty cutoff than a counterpart in the late 1960s. The change cannot be attributed to economic or other conditions unique to the period immediately surrounding 1982, since poverty appears to have deepened consistently through the entire period. But this is true only in cities—the deepening poverty was not present to the same extent for those living outside of urban counties.

Thus the chances that a poor person living in an urban county would exit from poverty increased somewhat between the late 1960s and the mid-1970s, but fell to well below the initial level by the early 1980s. Demographic changes over the period were, on balance, favorable to exiting from poverty; without them, the chances of exiting from urban poverty would have declined even more dramatically. However, the deepening poverty of the urban poor had the opposite effect, almost completely offsetting the favorable effects of the demographic changes.

The increasing persistence of poverty in urban counties was not matched outside those counties. However, after we adjusted for the changing demographic and economic conditions of the poor in the two areas, there proved to be little evidence of a differential trend.[21]

SUMMARY AND CONCLUSIONS

Of the three dimensions of urban poverty discussed by Bane and Jargowsky—underclass behavior, concentration, and persistence—we have chosen to focus on persistence. Persistently low living standards ought to be a prime policy concern, whether or not those who are persistently poor happen to live in high-poverty neighborhoods or exhibit "underclass" behavior.

Roughly two-fifths of the urban Americans who were

poor in the 1980 census can be characterized as persistently poor. The burdens of persistent urban poverty appear in many ways to be a simple extension of what census data have long revealed about single-year urban poverty: groups disproportionately represented among the single-year poor (e.g., blacks, the least educated, households headed by women) are even more heavily represented among the persistently poor. This suggests that long-run economic factors concentrate these disadvantaged groups at the lower end of the scale.

Three characteristics known to be prevalent among the single-year urban poor—little schooling, black ethnicity, and membership in a large household—were especially characteristic of the urban persistently poor. On the other hand, those who lived in a household headed by a white woman were a slightly smaller proportion of the persistently poor than of the one-year poor. This is consistent with evidence showing that the more favorable labor market and marital options open to white women result in shorter poverty spells for them than for black women.

Thus lack of schooling, skin color, and female headship are important correlates of persistent urban poverty, but the data failed to support other stereotypes of the urban persistently poor. For instance, only one in eight lived in a household headed by a never-married black woman—indeed, many more of the urban persistently poor are found in households headed by older, rather than younger, men and women.

Virtually all of the urban persistently poor lived in households headed by a person with at least one of four characteristics often used to define the "underclass"—female gender, dependence on welfare, lack of a job, and failure to complete high school—but so did half of the entire urban population. Roughly one in three persistently poor persons lived in households whose head exhibited all four of these characteristics. On the other hand, three-fifths of the persistently poor households shared one or more "deserving" characteristics—at least half-time work, spouse present in household, or head of household disabled or elderly.

Clearly one can find grounds for confirming—or refuting—many of the stereotypes that have been used to depict urban poverty. As a society, we should be concerned about a behavior-defined "underclass." But to focus exclusively on people with such characteristics would be to neglect the problems of a substantial number, probably a majority, of the urban persistently poor.

By the same token, most of the persistently poor lived outside of the most highly concentrated poverty areas. Only one in six persistently poor urban whites and just less than half of the persistently poor urban blacks live in ZIP Code areas with poverty rates above 30 percent; only one in ten of the urban persistently poor live in areas with poverty rates of 40 percent or more. Furthermore, although urban poverty may have become more concentrated since the 1960s, it is still true that a *nonpoor* black is almost as likely as a persistently poor one to live within a short walk of a high-poverty neighborhood.

Census figures show that poverty has become more prevalent in the nation's central cities since the late 1960s; our own analysis suggests that poverty has become more persistent as well. The chances that a poor person living in an urban county would exit from poverty have fallen substantially since the mid-1970s. Increasing inequality in income distribution has deepened the poverty of the urban poor, making it more difficult to exit; clearly we need to know why this inequality has increased. However, economic factors were to some extent counteracted by demographic shifts. Unfavorable demographic changes (such as the greater numbers of poor living in households headed by women) made it more difficult for the poor to leave poverty; but favorable changes (such as smaller family sizes and increased schooling of the heads of poor households) outweighed unfavorable ones, making the lessened chances of exiting from urban poverty less extreme.

In sum, despite much movement into and out of poverty among the urban population, a substantial number—perhaps two-fifths of those who were poor in any given year—are persistently poor. But they are not a single homogeneous group; they fit no single stereotype, either "deserving" or "underclass." Strategies for reducing persistent urban poverty must, to succeed, deal with this heterogeneity. The fact that nearly half of the persistently poor are children ought to be of grave concern. So should the fact that one-fifth are elderly—a finding that should give pause to those who have proclaimed victory in the battle against poverty among the elderly.

To deal with persistent poverty, we must move behind the simple descriptive statistics derived from Census Bureau "snapshots" of poverty. We must gain a better understanding of the dynamic processes that force some people to live in poverty for long periods, while others experience poverty only briefly, or not at all.

CHAPTER 6

Separate Societies: Have the Kerner Warnings Come True?

GARY ORFIELD

THE KERNER REPORT predicted that urban America was going to fragment into separate and unequal societies unless two basic goals were pursued with the greatest urgency: ending the racial inequality imposed by the ghetto system, and upgrading the inner-city communities that were in the midst of collapse. It acknowledged important efforts on both fronts in the sixties, such as the breaking of the Jim Crow system in southern cities and the urban programs of the Great Society, but said that much more needed to be done to avoid the further deterioration of race relations. Even in the great economic boom of the 1960s, the report warned that the problems of racial inequality and polarization were rapidly intensifying.

No major new efforts, however, were launched after the report was published in the spring of 1968. President Johnson pointed out in his autobiography that he was in a bitter struggle with an increasingly conservative Congress even to sustain his existing programs in the face of the rising costs of the Vietnam War.[1] The report came only months before the election of the Nixon administration, which was committed to a significant reduction of effort on both fronts. Nixon pursued an anti–civil-rights "Southern strategy" in his election campaign, and carried ten of the eleven southern states.[2]

With the election of Nixon and Reagan, whose administrations have set the basic social-policy agenda for the last twenty years, the country rejected the fundamental conclusions and recommendations of the Kerner Report. The issue of civil rights disappeared from national politics, and the idea that there was something fundamentally wrong with existing racial conditions, something that required strong governmental action, was rejected. Surveys showed the issue consistently low among white priorities, and reflected a very strong belief among white respondents that the problems of discrimination had been solved; indeed, many even felt that *whites* were now the victims of discrimination.

Presidential politics polarized on racial grounds, with four of the five elections since the Kerner Report won by the candidate who received virtually no black votes. With Republicans no longer competing for black votes, and with Democrats fighting for the support of white suburbanites, the Democrats had no incentive to raise issues that threatened to divide their constituency.

But even as the issue of urban racial discrimination disappeared from politics, the underlying economic conditions deteriorated sharply. A series of recessions, culminating in the worst economic crisis in a half-century, produced cycles of economic change and joblessness. The central cities came out of each cycle in worse shape, as more and more old employers failed, and new jobs went elsewhere. The shutdown of the older industrial facilities knocked out the first step toward economic mobility traditionally available to central-city youths with limited education. As unions were broken and forced into wage "givebacks," the economic situation of those who had made it to the first step worsened. Major new industrial or commercial enterprises were rarely located in minority communities.

In a period of political and intellectual attacks on government programs dealing with the problems of poverty and race, there was a strong tendency to blame those problems on minority culture and attitudes rather than on white institutions. If government intervention was futile or even counterproductive, argued the neoconservatives and the Nixon and Reagan administrations, it was best to do nothing—or even to undo what had been done earlier. If the problem was "defective" minority values, the answer was self-help and moral improvement.[3]

The Kerner Report concluded that deeply rooted processes growing out of a history of discrimination and racial fears demanded powerful interventions—or else racial separation would become more severe and its consequences worse. Have blacks—particularly those outside the middle class—indeed become further separated from white America over the past twenty years? And if so, what are the consequences?

In this chapter I will concentrate on the issue of ghettoization, not simply on that of economic inequality. Race is still the most basic divider in our cities, and racial inequalities cannot be solved through economic policies that do not directly address questions of ghettoization. Appropriate economic policies are essential but far from sufficient. It is vital to remember that the Kerner Report sought to explain severe problems that were becoming worse even in the midst of the most prosperous period in American history, when the overall unemployment rate was much lower than its present level.

In the 1980s, even in the metropolitan areas with the greatest economic growth and tightest overall labor markets, both the color line and racial inequalities persist. Whites who are poor are far less likely to be persistently poor, and rarely live or attend school in areas where the great majority of the community is poor. Millions of urban blacks, however, face profound racial and economic isolation from the mainstream society.

The evidence shows that the policies adopted during the Great Society were beneficial, but too weak to significantly change the segregation of our large cities, and they have, in any case, been seriously undermined over the past two decades. Indeed, inner-city blacks and Hispanics are more isolated than their predecessors, whose situation so worried the Kerner Commission.[4] To a considerable extent the residents of city ghettos are now living in separate and deteriorating societies, with separate economies, diverging family structures and basic institutions, and even growing linguistic separation within the core ghettos. The scale of their isolation by race, class, and economic situation is much greater than it was in the 1960s, impoverishment, joblessness, educational inequality, and housing insufficiency even more severe.

It is worth looking again at the fifteen cities that the Kerner Commission considered. If we examine the persistence and consequences of segregation in housing and schools in contemporary urban America, we can begin to assess the validity of the report's predictions.

Many liberals today underestimate the importance of the ghetto system and tend to see the urban race problem simply as an issue of class inequality that can be solved by nonracial social and economic policy. The growing liberal attack on the social policies of the Reagan administration has seen a revival of policy proposals paralleling some of the major recommendations of the Kerner Report for upgrading ghetto education and echoing its support for programs of subsidized housing and job training. The idea that market dynamics alone can solve society's problems and that government should not take an active role is under strong attack. There are now large popular majorities supporting the expansion of programs in education and health; and even in areas such as subsidized housing, the politics are beginning to change, as reflected in the enactment in 1987 of the first major housing bill of the decade. Congress has once again turned attention to the difficult task of welfare reform. If the terrible damage done to the federal tax base by the 1981 tax cuts can be repaired, there may be serious new policy initiatives. Still, most of these growing debates proceed as if the drastic problems of minority communities and institutions could be fixed without confronting their racial dimensions, or without forcing any basic changes in white institutions. Half of the message of the Kerner Report, the more troublesome half, has still been largely ignored.

The failure to refocus attention on the issue of the urban color line has been striking. One reason for this may be the rise of black political and administrative leadership in many central city institutions since the 1960s. This leadership often arises out of segregated districts and is swamped by overwhelming problems of short-term funding and program maintenance. When struggling to keep the school doors open or to cope with the effects of widespread housing abandonment (especially in a period of declining urban aid and shrinking tax bases), it is hard for local black leadership to find time to attack the larger system of racially defined, unequal schools and neighborhoods. Mayors and school boards who must go hat in hand to state capitals and Washington for funds to keep operating do not want to offend white policymakers who would respond strongly to threats to the suburban status quo. In some ways they are like the black administrators in the Jim Crow schools in the Old South: they must live on the largesse of white officials whose basic racial values they fear to challenge. The history of black communities shows that in conservative periods, when the possibilities shrink, political goals become more narrow: no longer do the communities attack the color line; all they can do is try to keep ghetto institutions functioning. We have been in such a situation; the new twist is that now the entire city or school system may be a black or minority institution.

Nor should it be surprising that white politicians are not raising the issues. Although white attitudes have improved on some important questions of race relations, surveys show that civil rights has been a very low priority for whites since the mid-1960s, with the brief exception of early 1968—the period of the Kerner Commission and the assassination of Martin Luther King. Many whites do not think government needs to do anything to change racial practices, and often strongly oppose concrete policies such as busing, scattered-site housing, and other attacks on the ghetto system. It is easier to assume that there is some solution that will work without attacking the color line, or to blame black values or "underclass culture" for the growing divergence between the core ghetto and the rest of society. During such a time, when political leaders ignore critical issues, serious investigation of unpopular issues is an especially important task.

HOUSING SEGREGATION

For blacks in the big cities, housing segregation is only slightly less severe than in the 1960s, and, for the large majority of blacks (those still in the rental market, compared to the almost two-thirds of whites who are in the ownership market), burden of housing costs is considerably worse. Housing segregation has changed importantly in ways that make it appear much less severe to whites and to a small sector of middle-class blacks, but the overall consequences of the ghetto system for working-class and poor blacks, and for the economic viability of central cities, have become more severe.

A study of sixty-four metropolitan areas, using 1980 census data, showed that 64 percent of blacks lived in low-income census tracts and that residents of such areas experienced no improvement in the very high level of segregation they knew between 1960 and 1980.[5] The overall small improvement in residential segregation levels was caused not by changes in the low-income areas but by the movement of more blacks into higher-income areas. This increasing suburbanization of middle-class blacks, in turn, reflected a growing income gap between city and suburban blacks.[6]

During the twenty-year period, there was only a very modest decline in the percentage of black households living in the most segregated tracts and a small increase of those living in areas less than 20 percent black. Thirty-five percent

TABLE 6.1 METROPOLITAN SEGREGATION, 1960–1980
Percentage of Whites in Census Tract of Typical Black

	1960	1980
Baltimore	24	26
Boston	50	40
Chicago	16	15
Cincinnati	33[a]	36
Cleveland	20	18
Detroit	27	20
Gary	20	19
Milwaukee	33	29
Newark	31[a]	27
New York	41	28
Philadelphia	31[a]	28
Pittsburgh	53	44
St. Louis	24	24
San Francisco	43	42
Washington, D.C.	25	30

Source: Schnare, "Residential Segregation by Race," Table B-1. Farley and Wilger, *Recent Changes in Residential Segregation*, Appendix

[a]1970 data; 1960 not available

of blacks lived in tracts that were 90 to 100 percent black in 1960 and 31 percent—now a much larger number of households—twenty years later. The proportion living in areas with a fifth or fewer black residents, the only areas with any significant likelihood of lasting integration, rose from 13 percent to 17 percent during this period.[7]

The overall national segregation trends have been measured by a number of researchers in somewhat different ways. In the fifteen cities chosen by the Kerner Commission for concentrated analysis, the segregation of blacks in the housing markets has not changed significantly. Other studies show that in the largest metropolitan areas, the urban centers in the Midwest, and those that have had relatively little recent residential growth, segregation levels are the highest. They also show that the largest metropolitan areas deserve a great deal of attention, because half of the U.S. black population resides in just twenty-five metropolitan areas.[8]

Housing markets do not, of course, end at city boundaries, and we need to consider changes across entire market areas. On a metropolitan level, the overall record of the United States is one of very little, if any, progress between 1960 and 1970 and modest gains in integration between 1970 and 1980. Segregation remained extremely high, however, and progress was smallest in the kind of metropolitan communities that were of greatest interest to the Kerner Commission: the older urban centers with the largest number and highest percentage of blacks. These areas had not only the most segregation but also the greatest racial inequality in job status, wealth, and level of education.[9] Racial differences appear to be greatest in areas with the largest and most restrictive ghetto systems.

Housing segregation is so serious because it is at the root of many other forms of segregation and inequality. It is increasingly linked to denial of opportunity for work, and it is the basis for the development of separate societies as feared by the Kerner Commission. Our courts have struck down as unconstitutional those laws that required overtly differential treatment by race; yet many other laws and policies that produce unequal opportunities—through distribution of services, of schooling, and so forth, on a geographic basis within areas of extreme segregation by race—are still seen as legitimate.

There is substantial evidence to show that contemporary residential segregation is not the result of different income levels. Although the income distribution of blacks and whites is very different, there is such a large overlap between high-wage blacks and low-wage whites, and such a wide range of housing costs in many areas, that virtually all parts of every metropolitan area studied would have a high level of integration if money were the sole explanation.[10] Statistics calculated for all areas with at least 250,000 black residents in 1980 showed that the level of segregation was just as high among blacks and whites from the highest income and education categories as it was for those in the lowest. "Blacks were thoroughly segregated from whites regardless of how much income they obtained or how many years they spent in school. The segregation score for families in the $50,000 and over range was just as high as the score for poverty level families."[11]

Recent studies have found strong evidence of continued discrimination by sales and rental agents, and of lack of conventional mortgage financing in black, Hispanic, and rapidly changing areas.[12] The history of segregation continues to inhibit successful integration in many respects. Minority families often bring limited market knowledge and considerable fears of white resistance to the housing search process, and whites fears—of the processes of ghettoization and economic and educational decline—lead to flight from integrated areas.[13]

There is virtually unanimous agreement that the fair-housing law adopted by Congress in 1968 has proved to be very weak and to lack any workable enforcement machinery. All secretaries of HUD since that time have recommended that it be strengthened, but action was blocked in Congress. Two decades after fair housing became law, the only thing HUD could do when a violation occurred was to ask the person discriminating to voluntarily stop and adopt better policies. Only a handful of cases are litigated each year in the entire country by the Justice Department. Under the Reagan administration, the Justice Department has asked for less compensation in those few cases that it has prosecuted.[14] A sign of a possible improvement in attitude was a 1988 agreement between civil-rights groups and the National Association of Realtors in favor of a modest strengthening of fair-housing enforcement powers.

Efforts to expand federal housing programs to foster fair housing have been abandoned during the 1980s. At the beginning of the Nixon administration (until the president reversed the policy) and through much of the Carter administration, there were efforts to tie eligibility for federal funding of suburbs to requirements for subsidized housing and civil-rights policies. The Carter administration had a combination of sanctions and incentives, together with a substantial subsidized-housing construction program, which made some progress possible. The Reagan administration ended the incentives, virtually eliminated new housing construction for subsidized families, and ended civil-rights enforcement in the Community Development Block Grant program.

CONTEMPORARY CONSEQUENCES OF SEGREGATION

Even if there were no other direct consequences of residential segregation and ghetto expansion, the discrimination and denial of choice would justify an active public policy to assure equal opportunity. In fact, however, there are large and very important consequences. Residential segregation produces segregated schools and, as the current data cited later in this chapter show, integegated schools are very likely to be much better on every index measured. Segregated minority areas experience disinvestment and do not receive a reasonable share of housing finance.[15] When compared in terms of average income, occupation, education, and percentage of population in poverty, a recent study showed that areas that were all-black before 1970 fared worst, followed by those that had rapidly become black, followed by those that had changed more slowly. Of the multiracial neighborhoods, by far the best conditions were found in those that were stably integrated.[16]

One of the most important consequences of residential isolation in the postindustrial cities is that as jobs are increasingly concentrated in the suburban periphery, where they are very hard to reach from the inner city, particularly for the large proportion of black households without reliable cars, the ghetto tends to become an even more isolated, separate economy. A recent study of metropolitan Atlanta found rapid economic growth since 1980, but with extreme contrasts between those virtually all-white outlying areas and the black central city and inner suburban areas. Job growth was many times higher in the segregated white areas, which were pulling in workers from other parts of the country, while black joblessness remained high.[17] National studies by John Kasarda at the University of North Carolina have documented a pattern of serious "spatial mismatch" between job location and minority residence across the United States.[18]

There are other broad trends in housing for urban blacks that may be partially explained by residential segregation and the unequal mortgage funding associated with it. There are still far fewer black homeowners than white, even after controlling for differences in income. Since equity in a home is the only substantial wealth of most families, this helps account for the fact that the typical white family had eleven times more wealth than the typical black family in the mid-1980s, a gap dramatically larger than the black-white income and employment gaps. The shortage of subsidized housing, and the fact that most black children are now being born in single-parent families—and are likely to live in poverty or near-poverty—means that a large proportion of black youth will grow up in households facing a constant housing crisis that severely limits their access to decent schools and the growing part of the job market. The typical black family below poverty, in two recently studied metropolitan areas, is now paying three-fourths of its cash income for housing expenses if it lives in private housing. This rental burden has been rising.[19] To reverse these trends there must be greater access to integrated housing areas for upper-income blacks, and a more aggressive program of subsidized housing, in areas with good schools and job growth, for poor black families.

SEGREGATION IN THE SCHOOLS

Educational segregation perpetuates inequality across generations by providing far weaker and less effective training for young blacks and Hispanics than for whites. Current research by the University of Chicago's Metropolitan Opportunity Project on large American metropolitan areas, shows an extremely strong pattern of educational segregation for blacks in both cities and suburbs, as well as rapidly increasing segregation for Hispanics, particularly in central cities. The percentage of black and Hispanic students in a school indicates a great deal about both the economic background of the students and the performance levels of the school. Minority high schools, almost without exception, have large numbers of low-income students; there are no predominantly low-income white high schools in the metropolitan areas studied. In other words, if you know only the racial composition of a high school, you can predict its percentage of poor children, the average achievement scores, dropout rates, college entrance exam scores, etc. with a dismayingly high probability. I will discuss this data after examining the basic trends in school segregation in the Kerner Report cities.

Blacks outside the South are very highly concentrated in large cities and large metropolitan areas. (The South has had the largest number of integrated public schools since 1970.) The cities and areas studied by the Kerner Commission still have a dramatically disproportionate influence on the conditions of blacks in the United States. These fifteen central cities had 1.47 million black students in 1980, 23 percent of the national total, and their suburban rings doubtless had several percent more. In 1986–87, nine times as high a share of black as white students went to school in the nation's twenty-five largest central-city districts. These districts were critical for blacks, but almost irrelevant for whites.

The cities studied by the Kerner Commission all had predominantly minority school districts by 1980. Only three of the systems had more than 40 percent white students left, and most had more than three-fourths nonwhite students. By

TABLE 6.2 PERCENTAGE OF WHITE ENROLLMENT IN KERNER COMMISSION CITIES' SCHOOL DISTRICTS IN 1968 AND 1980

	1968	1980
Baltimore	35	21
Boston	68	35
Chicago	38	19
Cincinnati	57	42
Cleveland	43	28
Detroit	39	12
Gary	29	8
Milwaukee	73	45
Newark	18	9
New York	44	26
Philadelphia	39	29
Pittsburgh	60	48
St. Louis	36	21
San Francisco	41	17
Washington, D.C.	6	4

Source: Orfield, *Public School Desegregation*, Appendix B.

1980 there were very few large city school systems left in the United States with white majorities, and virtually all cities continued to experience ongoing decline in white students, whether or not they had any desegregation plan.[20]

Enrollment changes reflected the broader changes in the demography of young families in metropolitan America affecting the entire nation. Between 1968 and 1986, the number of white students in American public schools dropped 16 percent, while the number of blacks increased 5 percent, and the number of Hispanics soared 103 percent. This was not caused by any substantial shift to private education but was a reflection of the country's changing population structure. These changes meant that segregation affected a growing

TABLE 6.3 PERCENTAGE OF WHITE STUDENTS IN THE SCHOOL OF THE TYPICAL BLACK STUDENT IN HIGHLY INTEGRATED METROPOLITAN AREAS, FALL 1984

City	Percentage of White Students
Tampa–St. Petersburg, Fla.	66.3
Wilmington, Del.	65.7
Louisville, Ky.	65.43
Greenville, S.C.	61.1
Greensboro, N.C.	57.6
Nashville, Tenn.	55.3
Orlando, Fla.	51.1

sector of the nation's total pupils, and that desegregation in predominantly white schools would become steadily more difficult as the proportion of whites dropped and the population centers for young blacks and whites moved farther and farther apart in sprawling metropolitan areas.

The Supreme Court's 1974 Detroit decision, *Milliken* v. *Bradley,* blocked desegregation of city and suburban children in one of the nation's largest metropolitan areas. Lower federal courts had found that the segregation was the result of a history of unconstitutional local and state actions and had concluded that no remedy was possible within an overwhelmingly black city. The Supreme Court blocked the broader metropolitan plan and required the implementation of a plan within the city. Justice Thurgood Marshall and the other dissenters in the 5–4 decision predicted that such a plan would be futile, given the long-established demographic trends in the city.[21] Experience proved them right. According to the statistics for the 1984–85 school year, metropolitan Detroit is now one of the nation's most segregated metropolitan areas. The 9 percent of whites in schools attended by the

TABLE 6.4 **SEGREGATION OF BLACK STUDENTS, 1968–1984**

	Percentage in Predominantly Minority Schools	Percentage in 90–100% Minority Schools
1968	73.6	64.3
1972	63.6	38.7
1980	62.9	33.2
1984	63.5	33.2

Source: Orfield, *Public School Desegregation*; Orfield and Monfort, "Are American Schools Resegregating?"

typical black student in metro Detroit compares badly to white averages of 60 percent or more in the schools of typical black students in some southern metropolitan areas where city-suburban busing plans have been in effect since the 1971 Supreme Court *Swann* decision (see Table 6.4). Many large southern metropolitan areas have had city-suburban desegregation plans since the early 1970s, and some have had no segregated schools for years. The two major merger orders of the 1970s, creating city-suburban mandatory desegregation in metropolitan Wilmington and Louisville, radically lowered segregation for those entire states. These plans have been far more stable and have produced a much higher level of integration than those limited to central cities.

There has been no progress in school desegregation on a national level since the Supreme Court's decision in the Detroit case,[22] which created an overwhelming barrier to city-suburban desegregation in the largest cities. None of the cities covered by the Kerner Report have succeeded in winning such a plan. The two that sued their suburbs and carried out a comprehensive legal battle, St. Louis and Milwaukee, both ended up signing settlements with suburban districts in the 1980s that permitted a substantial number of blacks to

TABLE 6.5 PERCENTAGE OF WHITE STUDENTS IN THE SCHOOL OF THE TYPICAL BLACK STUDENT IN SELECTED METROPOLITAN AREAS, 1984

City	Percentage of White Students
Baltimore	16
Boston	32
Chicago	9
Cincinnati	32
Cleveland	22
Detroit	9
Milwaukee	35
Newark	9
New York	11
Philadelphia	17
St. Louis	16
San Francisco	18
Washington, D.C.	24

Source: Office for Civil Rights data.

transfer to the suburbs but left many segregated black schools behind. The Supreme Court's Detroit decision, together with the almost total failure of state and national leadership on the issue, has left the country without tools to deal with the vast disparity between minority central-city school districts and schools in white suburbs.

Adequate data were not collected in most of these metropolitan areas to compute the earlier segregation levels. Those for which comparative 1970 and 1984 data are available, however, show a tendency toward declining contact between black and white students. In metropolitan Baltimore the number of whites in the school of the typical black student dropped 3 percent from an already very low level in the fourteen-year period. In metropolitan San Francisco–Oakland and metropolitan Washington, D.C., the drop was 9 percent. (The figures for Hispanics show much more rapid increases in segregation.)

School segregation would be of far less concern if it were not associated with inequality. In spite of large resources and some real progress in early-childhood education and teaching of basic skills in the central-city minority schools, there is pervasive inequality. Recent examinations of schools in four metropolitan areas show an extremely high relationship in the mid-1980s between the race of a school, its level of poverty, and educational outcomes. A great many black students, and a rapidly growing number of Hispanic students, are trapped in schools where more than half drop out, where the average achievement level of those who remain is so low that there is little serious pre-collegiate instruction, where pre-collegiate courses and counselors are much less available, and which only prepare students for the least competitive colleges.[23]

Recent studies of schools in the city and suburbs of metropolitan Chicago, Los Angeles, Atlanta, and Milwaukee show fundamental differences between minority and white schools and show an extremely high correlation between the percentage of minority students and the percentage of low-income students. These correlations are stunningly similar in four very different metropolitan areas. Race and class are so intertwined in the schools, in other words, that it makes little sense to talk about them in isolation from one another. The relationship between race (or income level) and achievement scores is similarly powerful. White schools are not low-income schools, and they have dramatically higher achievement levels. These statistical relationships are extremely strong. There are also clear relationships between race and dropout levels, attendance levels, college entrance test taking, and many other aspects of schooling. Some of the only significant exceptions to this in the cities studied are the magnet schools, where the race-class linkage is often broken through procedures or entrance requirements that screen out most low-income children.[24] In spite of the fine work of many minority educators, black and Hispanic schools remain extremely different from white schools in ways that are decisive for the preparation of students for work and college.

WHAT CAN BE DONE?

After twenty years of ignoring the Kerner Report's warnings about civil rights and race relations, can anything still be done that is likely to have a positive effect? Some analysts seem to argue that racial separation has become irreversible, or that there is simply nothing we know of that will make it better. Fortunately, the facts are different.

We have learned a great deal since the Kerner Report about the possibilities for building an integrated society. Court orders, experiments of various types, alternative local leadership, demographic and sociological research, and community efforts to cope with threatening conditions have all taught us something about the possibilities for a successful integrationist policy. Working examples have emerged that could become the models for new policies.

Large-scale school desegregation works and is relatively stable over long periods of time. School integration appears to have effects that go far beyond test scores—it seems to increase the probability of attending college and to positively affect outcomes such as type of college, college major, type of employment as an adult, and likelihood of living in an integrated neighborhood as an adult. The Kerner Commission's call for a serious effort of desegregation was very much to the point.

Many large southern metropolitan areas have had city-suburban desegregation plans since the early 1970s, and some have had no segregated schools for years. The two major merger orders of the 1970s, creating city-suburban mandatory desegregation in metropolitan Wilmington and Louisville, radically lowered segregation for those entire states. These plans have been far more stable and have produced a much higher level of integration than those limited to central cities. Among the largest U.S. school districts, most of those losing white enrollment the least rapidly from 1967 to 1986 had massive city-suburban busing plans.[25]

During the 1980s there has been a very important change in the way desegregation plans are designed and implemented. The first round of urban plans to follow the Supreme Court's busing decision in 1971 were primarily in the South. They were limited to single districts (some of which contained entire urban counties), were almost wholly mandatory, and were developed so quickly that there was seldom an opportunity to plan and implement major educational changes until after the order was in place. Almost all of the new plans of the last decade, in sharp contrast, have important educational improvements, and many involve a great expansion of parental choices in magnet schools, special programs, and voluntary interdistrict exchanges. Under many of the newer orders, the state governments have been obliged to fund large compensatory efforts to upgrade inner-city minority schools and students.

In other words, some courts, and many state and local officials and civil-rights litigators, are thinking about how to make the Kerner Report's prescriptions more acceptable to middle-class families by introducing a much broader range of well-developed educational options to meet the special needs of more children.

This development probably helps account for the substantial increase in public support in the 1980s for desegregation plans that require busing. Americans under thirty now support such plans, as do college students and more than two-thirds of the families whose children have actually been bussed for desegregation purposes.[26]

Fair-housing program research also shows the possibility of real progress against ghettoization when there are supportive public policies. The level of segregation did decline significantly between 1970 and 1980 in metropolitan areas where a large amount of new housing was built, and where there were relatively small black populations.

There are other effective techniques, such as fair-housing counseling, that will increase housing-market knowledge and, therefore, the range of choices for minority families. Research shows that people who live in stably integrated areas find it a positive experience, and the key may be programs that diminish both the fear of resegregation and the likelihood that it will recur. Significant numbers of communities have learned how to educate and integrate successfully, even in the midst of some of the nation's most segregated housing markets. There is information that shows that, where there is widespread school desegregation, residential integration increases. And we have examples in both Maryland and Colorado of substantial housing development intentionally planned to be integrated—and coming out as planned. In Chicago, a program successfully moved hundreds of black public-assistance families into units in white apartment buildings in outer suburbia. In Yonkers, the federal courts are now implementing the first combined school and housing desegregation order, which was recently approved by the Court of Appeals. These experiments, often carried out with no federal support, show the possibilities of even better outcomes.

During the past two decades, the predictions of the Kerner Report have been borne out in the large metropolitan areas on which it focused. The condition of inner-city black families and communities is even more precarious and more separated from mainstream American society than it was then. Under the Nixon administration the country abandoned its focus on changing the ghetto system. The Reagan administration has also weakened many of the compensatory programs intended to keep ghetto institutions viable and to provide access to the middle-class society and economy for some central-city blacks. It is very important to realize that the warnings of the Kerner Report are coming true, that the consequences are even greater in a society where the white majority is shrinking rapidly, and that—most importantly—we are not helpless in the face of these trends. A great deal has been learned about what can work and how it can be done. We need to refocus energy and commitment toward the goal of becoming a more integrated and far more equal society.

CHAPTER 7

The Ghetto Underclass and the Changing Structure of Urban Poverty

WILLIAM JULIUS WILSON,
ROBERT APONTE,
JOLEEN KIRSCHENMAN, AND
LOÏC J. D. WACQUANT

INNER-CITY NEIGHBORHOODS IN the nation's large metropolises have undergone rapid social deterioration since the Kerner Report was released in 1968. The report concluded that among the leading causes of the racial strife visited upon urban America during the previous four summers were the continued exclusion of great numbers of blacks from the benefits of economic progress, the concentration of poor blacks in major cities, and the restriction of blacks to ghettos, where segregation and poverty converged to destroy opportunity and enforce failure.[1]

Twenty years later, we find that these same conditions are central to the problem of urban poverty, only in a more aggravated form; the ghetto, the media say, has gone "from bad to worse.[2] Not even the most pessimistic observers" of the social scene in the late 1960s anticipated the massive breakdown of social institutions and the dramatic increases in rates of social dislocation that have since swept through the ghettos. The term "ghetto underclass," rarely used two decades ago, is now frequently invoked in both popular and scholarly discussions of the growing social problems—crime, family disruption, teenage pregnancy, drugs, joblessness, failing schools, and dilapidated housing—that plague those who live in today's inner city.

A particularly worrisome trend, though one that has received little attention, is the *increasing concentration of urban poverty* and the *institutional transformation of the ghetto* that has come with it. Thus, while poverty as a whole has become a predominantly urban phenomenon in the United States over the last thirty years, most of the growth of metropolitan poverty itself has occurred in the central city. Between 1969 and 1985, the number of poor individuals living in central cities increased by 77 percent (from 8 to 14.2 million), while the proportion of inner-city residents below the official poverty line rose from 12.7 percent to 19 percent. At the same time, the number of poor individuals in urban poverty areas (census tracts where at least 20 percent of the population is below the official poverty level) nearly doubled between 1974 and 1985 (from 4.1 million to 7.8 million). By 1985, the poor living in the urban poverty areas accounted for a clear majority of all the central-city poor in America.

This significant increase in the concentration of urban poverty paralleled a geographic spread of poverty. In this chapter, we will use data from 1970 to 1980 to focus first on changes in the ten largest metropolises of the country, and second on changes in Chicago's inner city. We will then address two fundamental questions: Why has the concentration of poverty in inner-city neighborhoods increased so rapidly in recent years? What are the consequences of such highly concentrated poverty for the social organization of, and life in, these neighborhoods?

THE GROWING CONCENTRATION OF URBAN POVERTY

In the fifty largest cities in the United States, the number of persons living in poverty areas increased by more than 20 percent between 1970 and 1980, even as the total population of these cities decreased by 5 percent.[3] In effect, poverty has become primarily a big-city, central-city phenomenon. Let us begin our analysis by closely examining population and social changes in the ten largest cities in the nation as of 1970: New York, Chicago, Los Angeles, Philadelphia, Detroit, Houston, Baltimore, Dallas, Cleveland, and Indianapolis.[4] By 1980, these ten cities alone contained over half of the country's entire poverty population, and a full 40 percent of all black poor in the fifty largest American cities. By focusing on them, we can trace the nature and extent of the transformation of the inner-city neighborhoods and see the changing structure of urban poverty.

The ten largest cities lost 1.5 million residents (a drop of 7 percent) between 1970 and 1980. The drop was due mainly to the exodus of whites; the white population decreased by a fourth, from 15.5 to 11.6 million, while the number of blacks edged up half a million to 6.3 million and

TABLE 7.1 POVERTY AND POPULATION CHANGE BY RACE AND HISPANIC ORIGIN IN THE TEN LARGEST CENTRAL CITIES, 1970–1980

	1970	%	1980	%	% Change
TOTAL POPULATION	**21,713,000**	**100**	**20,164,000**	**100**	**−7.2**
Poverty Population	3,174,000	14.6	3,777,000	18.7	+19.0
Population in Poverty Areas	5,574,000	25.7	7,484,000	37.1	+34.3
Population in Extreme Poverty Areas	918,000	4.2	2,048,000	10.2	+123.1
WHITES: TOTAL POPULATION	**15,484,000**	**100**	**11,643,000**	**100**	**−24.9**
Poverty Population	1,646,000	10.6	1,322,000	11.4	−19.7
Population in Poverty Areas	2,006,000	12.9	2,089,000	17.9	+4.1
Population in Extreme Poverty Areas	233,000	1.5	336,000	2.9	+44.2
BLACKS: TOTAL POPULATION	**5,870,000**	**100**	**6,333,000**	**100**	**+7.9**
Poverty Population	1,474,000	25.1	1,832,200	28.9	+24.3
Population in Poverty Areas	3,459,000	58.9	4,156,000	65.6	+20.1
Population in Extreme Poverty Areas	676,000	11.5	1,378,000	21.5	+103.8

TABLE 7.1 *(Continued)*

	1970	%	1980	%	% Change
HISPANICS: TOTAL POPULATION	2,297,000	100	3,132,000	100	+36.3
Poverty Population	526,000	22.8	913,000	29.1	+73.6
Population in Poverty Areas	1,091,000	47.5	1,816,000	58.0	+66.4
Population in Extreme Poverty Areas	173,000	7.5	516,000	16.5	+198.3

Sources: U.S. Bureau of the Census. 1973. *Census of Population: 1970,* Subject Reports, "Low Income Areas in Large Cities." PC(2)-9B.

———. 1985b. *Census of Population: 1980,* Subject Reports, "Poverty Areas in Large Cities." PC80-2-8D.

the number of Hispanics increased by over a third to 3.2 million (see Table 7.1). As a result, the racial composition of these cities has shifted from one largely dominated by whites (71.3 percent in 1970) to one that is polarized between the dominant white population and minorities (blacks and Hispanics made up 43 percent of the total in 1980).

The changing racial composition of these central cities is strongly linked to significant shifts in the poverty population. Despite the decreased population of the cities, the number of persons in poverty increased by 19 percent (from 3.2 to 3.8 million), due solely to the growth of poverty among blacks (up 24 percent, from 1.5 to 1.8 million) and Hispanics (up 73 percent, from 0.5 to 0.9 million). The number of poor whites over this period decreased by 20 percent, from 1.6 to 1.3 million. Furthermore, the poverty rate among whites in these cities remained around 10 percent between 1970 and 1980, while it increased among blacks (from 25 to 29 percent) and among Hispanics (from 23 to 29 percent). Hence, in 1970 roughly the same number of poor whites as poor blacks resided in the top ten central cities; by 1980 the number of poor blacks exceeded the number of poor whites. Indeed, the racial gap was even greater than these figures suggest: when we compare blacks with non-Hispanic whites, we see that the poor population of these cities in 1980 is composed of nearly twice as many blacks as non-Hispanic whites (1.8 million compared with just under 1 million). Not surprisingly, the increase in poverty in these ten cities went hand in hand with a rise in the number of families receiving public assistance. In 1970, 8.4 percent of the families received public assistance, but by 1980 this proportion had climbed to 15 percent (7.9 percent among whites, 27.3 percent among blacks, and 22.9 percent among Hispanics).

Changes in total population, poverty population, and the proportion of publicly assisted families in these ten central cities have all been more pronounced within *poverty areas.* In particular, racial differences have become sharper, and markedly more so as the level of poverty in these areas rises. From 1970 to 1980, poverty areas in these cities witnessed a 34 percent increase in total population (from 5.6 to 7.5 million), including a 66 percent leap in the Hispanic population, a 20 percent rise in the black population, and a meager 4 percent increase in the non-Hispanic white population. It is reasonable to assume that all of the growth in the white population was accounted for by Hispanic whites. When Hispanic whites are distinguished from non-Hispanic whites in the 1980 census data, we see that only 32 percent of the latter were poverty-area residents, whereas a large majority

(66 percent) of blacks and more than half of all Hispanics (58 percent) lived in poverty tracts at that time. Finally, in these poverty areas, the proportion of families receiving public assistance rose from 24.9 percent in 1970 to 29.5 percent in 1980. Since this growth occurred among blacks (from 24.5 to 34.9 percent) and Hispanics (from 26.7 to 31.2 percent), while it remained stable at about 20 percent among whites, one can reasonably conclude that welfare receipt decreased among non-Hispanic whites during the decade.

But it is in the *extreme-poverty areas*—census tracts where the rate of poverty exceeds 40 percent—that these changes have been most spectacular. There, the total number of residents doubled in one decade to slightly over 2 million in 1980. The number of Hispanics in these areas increased threefold (from 173,000 to 516,000), the number of blacks shot up by 104 percent (from 676,000 to 1,378,000), and the number of whites grew by 44 percent. Here again, the *enormous racial discrepancies* are remarkable. In 1980, less than 2 percent of all non-Hispanic whites in these ten cities lived in extreme-poverty areas—contrasted with 16.5 percent of all Hispanics and 21 percent of all blacks. As expected, extreme-poverty areas have borne the steepest rise in the proportion of families receiving public assistance, from 34 percent in 1970 to 45 percent in 1980.

Finally, the total poor population in the ten largest cities was *more concentrated* in poverty areas, and particularly in extreme-poverty areas, in 1980 than it was a decade before. Indeed, the poorer the area, the faster the poverty population grew over this period. Consequently, the proportion of poor people residing in non-poor areas decreased from 45 percent in 1970 to 32 percent in 1980, while the proportion residing in extreme-poverty areas doubled from 13 to 27 percent.

TABLE 7.2 DISTRIBUTION OF POVERTY POPULATION BY TYPE OF POVERTY AREA AND GROUP, TEN LARGEST CITIES, 1980

	Total	Non-Poverty 0–19%		Low Poverty 20–29%		High Poverty 30–39%		Extreme Poverty 40%+	
	N	N	%	N	%	N	%	N	%
TOTAL	**3,777,000**	**1,199,000**	**31.7**	**790,000**	**20.9**	**772,000**	**20.4**	**1,016,000**	26.9
Whites	1,322,000	759,000	57.4	269,000	20.3	150,000	11.4	144,000	10.9
Blacks	1,832,000	294,000	16.0	372,000	20.3	478,000	26.1	688,000	37.6
Hispanics	913,000	207,000	22.7	222,000	24.3	212,000	23.2	272,000	29.8
Non-Hisp. Whites	960,000	650,000	67.7	175,000	18.2	74,000	7.7	61,000	6.4

Source: same as Table 7.1.

Nonetheless, as presented in Table 7.2, a substantial majority (68 percent) of all poor non-Hispanic whites lived in non-poor areas in 1980. In sharp contrast, in that same year only 16 percent of all poor blacks and 23 percent of all poor Hispanics were nonpoverty-area residents. While most poor blacks and most poor Hispanics lived in high- to extreme-poverty areas in 1980 (62 and 53 percent respectively), poor non-Hispanic whites rarely resided in such areas (14.1 percent). In sum, it is important to note, first, that in the nation's ten largest cities, poor non-Hispanic whites were six times less likely than poor blacks to live in an extremely poor neighborhood, and five times less likely than poor Hispanics; and, second, that whereas *one* out of every five poor blacks in these cities lived in extreme-poverty areas in 1970, by 1980 nearly *two* out of every five did so. It is crucial, then, to recognize racial differences in type of neighborhood of residence when drawing comparisons between poor urban whites and poor urban minorities.

This brief analysis reveals several significant trends: a marked increase, in both relative and absolute terms, of urban poverty despite a net loss of population; an even sharper rise in the population living in poverty and extreme-poverty areas; an increasing concentration over time of the poor in the poorest sections of these cities; and widely divergent patterns of concentration between whites and minorities. Several interrelated processes account for this differential growth in the size and distribution of the poverty population in the inner city. In the next section we will examine these processes in some detail, using data from the city of Chicago as a case study.

THE SOCIAL TRANSFORMATION OF THE INNER CITY: THE CASE OF CHICAGO

Chicago is instructive to study because, there, many of the trends documented above are even more pronounced, due to the high level of racial segregation and the predominance of industrial activity that have long typified this city. From 1970 to 1980, Chicago lost about one-tenth of its population, which has now stabilized at around 3 million, while its poor population went up by one-fourth—from 483,000 to 601,000. The population increased by 43 percent in poverty areas and 136 percent in extreme-poverty areas. In 1980, one in ten white residents of Chicago was poor, while one of every four Hispanics, and one of every three blacks, lived below the official poverty level. Again, the growth and concentration of poverty primarily affected minority residents.

Based on the percentage of households with incomes below the poverty line, and using community areas as the basic unit, our analysis shows that there has been both a significant *geographic expansion* of poverty between 1970 and 1980 and a substantial *rise in the incidence of poverty* in the poorest of these urban areas—most notably in the black ghetto neighborhoods of the South and West Sides.[5] In 1970, only sixteen of Chicago's seventy-seven community areas had rates of poverty above 20 percent; twenty-five did so by 1980. Similarly, in 1970 only eight of these community areas had rates of poverty above 30 percent, and only one had a rate exceeding 40 percent; by 1980, 14 had reached the 30 percent mark, including two with rates in excess of 50 percent.

Let us now focus on two of the intertwined processes at

TABLE 7.3 POVERTY AND POPULATION CHANGE IN CHICAGO'S POOR COMMUNITY AREAS, 1970–1980

City	Poverty Rate		% Change 1970–80	
	1970 %	1980 %	TOTAL POPULATION	POOR FAMILIES
1 Oakland	44.4	60.9	−8.4	+38.1
2 Grand Boulevard	37.4	51.4	−32.9	−7.1
3 Near West Side	34.7	48.9	−27.2	+5.1
4 Riverdale	37.8	44.8	−9.8	+16.0
5 Washington Park	28.2	43.2	−30.6	+1.2
6 Near South Side	37.2	42.7	−17.4	−20.9
7 Douglas	30.2	42.6	−13.5	+9.4
8 East Garfield Park	32.4	40.3	−39.5	−24.0
9 North Lawndale	30.0	39.9	−35.1	−10.0
10 West Garfield Park	24.5	37.2	−30.1	+3.8
11 Englewood	24.3	35.8	−34.2	−1.3
12 Fuller Park	27.0	34.5	−29.9	−0.4
13 Woodlawn	26.5	32.3	−32.5	−32.0
14 West Englewood	12.0	29.4	+0.3	+125.2
15 West Town	19.4	27.2	−22.7	+5.6
16 Near North Side	22.2	26.2	−4.4	+6.5
17 Humboldt Park	13.0	25.9	+10.0	+75.8
18 Armour Square	19.3	23.4	−4.5	+19.0
19 Lower West Side	15.5	22.6	+1.0	+42.6
20 Uptown	15.8	22.6	−13.9	+6.5
21 Greater Grand Crossing	14.1	22.4	−16.9	+30.0
22 Austin	8.1	21.8	+7.8	+160.0
23 New City	10.2	21.9	−8.2	+81.8
24 South Shore	7.8	20.8	−3.9	+136.9
25 South Lawndale	11.7	19.5	+19.6	+72.7
26 Kenwood	24.1	20.0	−8.4	−34.6

Source: Chicago Fact Book Consortium, *Local Community Fact Book: Chicago Metropolitan Area.* Chicago: Chicago Review Press, 1984.

work here: the increase in the absolute number of poor families living in these poor neighborhoods, and the disproportionate outmigration of nonpoor residents. As shown in Table 7.3, in the ten years between 1970 and 1980, twenty-five of the twenty-six poverty community areas of Chicago (all but five of which are all or predominantly black) experienced notable increases in their rate of family poverty, while eighteen of them recorded a net growth in the number of poor families. Six had increases ranging from 1 to 15 percent; six had increases between 15 and 50 percent; and six had increases that exceeded 70 percent, including three that recorded a rise in the 125 to 160 percent range. Significantly in most cases this absolute growth in poverty took place despite depopulation: of these eighteen community areas, only four had a larger total population in 1980 than in 1970, and in each, the increase in the number of poor families clearly outpaced that of the overall population. In West Englewood, where the population remained roughly the same (but went from 48 to 98 percent black), the number of poor families shot up 125 percent; in Humboldt Park, a predominantly Hispanic area, the number of poor families grew eight times faster than the number of residents; in South Lawndale, a white ethnic enclave becoming increasingly Hispanic, the same was true; in Austin, a section of the West Side that went from one-third black to all-black, this ratio was twenty-three to one. Moreover, of the seven community areas that experienced a decline in the absolute number of poor families, all but one—the Near South Side, which has been undergoing partial gentrification—incurred even greater losses in total population. Grand Boulevard, for instance, which is the historic heart of Chicago's black ghetto, lost 7 percent of its poor families but a third of its total population; North Lawndale, an all-black neighborhood on Chicago's West Side, lost 10 percent of its poor families but 35 percent of its residents; Englewood, another all-black neighborhod on the South Side, had declines of 1 percent and 30 percent, respectively.

That the poorest community areas in Chicago experienced an increase in the number of poor families despite a substantial reduction in the total population indicates two things. First, the growing concentration of poverty in these neighborhoods is related to the *large outmigration of nonpoor* individuals and families. As shown in Table 7.3, the fourteen black community areas with poverty rates of 30 percent and more in 1980 had a net aggregate outmigration of 39 percent, losing a total of 228,000 persons, including 195,000 blacks. The exodus of nonpoor (i.e., working) families from these areas has left behind a more highly concentrated poverty population, contributing to the aggravation of social and economic conditions in these neighborhoods and to the geographic spread of poverty as well. Second, the increase in the absolute number of poor families is also a function of the *sharp growth in joblessness* during the 1970s. Figure 7.1 shows the simultaneous increase in poverty and unemployment in Chicago's poorest inner-city neighborhoods.[6] The strong connection between poverty and unemployment is also shown in Figure 7.2, which exhibits a clear linear relationship that places the communities of the historic Black Belt farther out on the scattergram than the partly gentrified white areas and the predominantly Hispanic sections of the city (such as parts of West Town, Humboldt Park, and the Lower West Side).

Just as a rise in unemployment is closely related to an increase in poverty, so, too, it is associated with the growth of female-headed families, as shown in Figure 7.3, which also reveals the gap between black ghetto neighborhoods and

FIGURE 7.1 JOINT INCREASE IN POVERTY AND UNEMPLOYMENT FOR SELECTED CHICAGO COMMUNITY AREAS, 1970–80

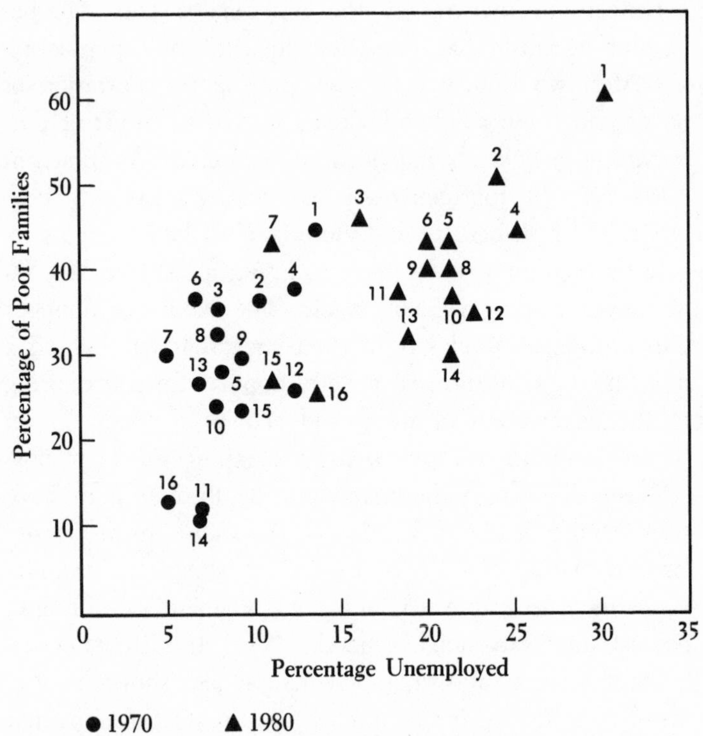

other poor areas of Chicago observed in Figure 7.2. We will argue later that increasing joblessness has its most devastating effect precisely in these most highly concentrated poverty areas.[7] But let us first document in greater detail the extent of these social transformations of the inner city, including the staggering increase in joblessness, by focusing on three of Chicago's poorest black neighborhoods.

FIGURE 7.2 DISTRIBUTION OF POVERTY COMMUNITY AREAS BY PERCENTAGE OF POOR FAMILIES AND PERCENTAGE OF PEOPLE UNEMPLOYED, 1980

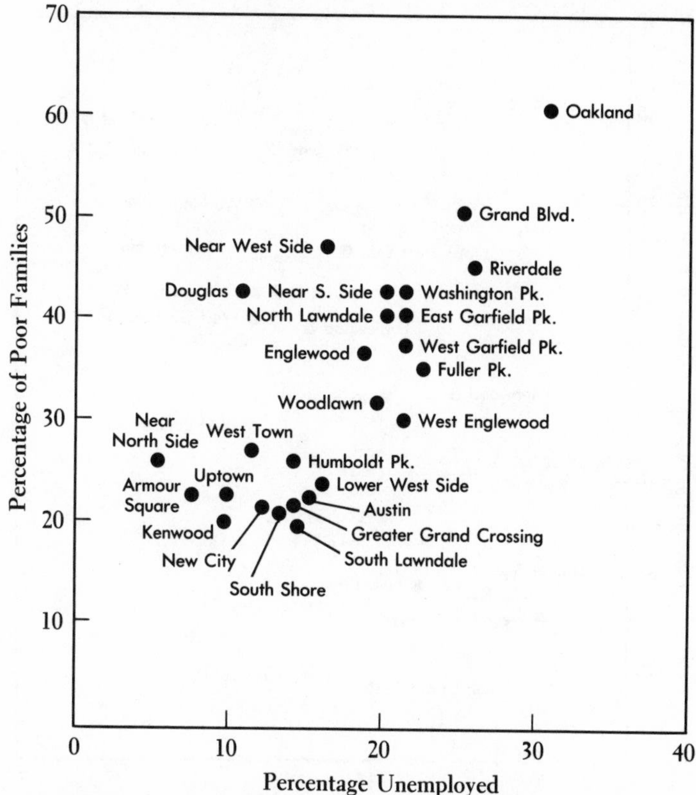

Oakland, Grand Boulevard, and Washington Park, three all-black areas located on Chicago's South Side, are part of the historic Black Belt. In 1980 they were respectively the poorest, second-poorest, and fifth-poorest neighborhoods of the city (as measured by the proportion of families below the federal poverty line), with poverty rates ranging as high as 40 to 60 percent. These areas have fared considerably worse than

FIGURE 7.3 DISTRIBUTION OF POVERTY COMMUNITY AREAS BY PERCENTAGE OF PEOPLE UNEMPLOYED AND PERCENTAGE OF FEMALE-HEADED FAMILIES, 1980.

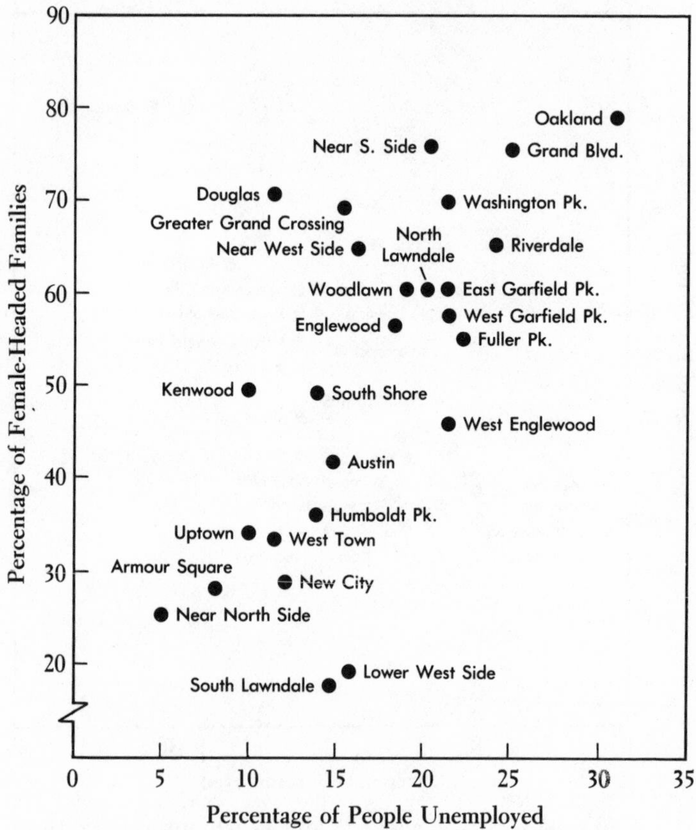

the city as a whole since 1950, with a dramatic worsening of conditions during the decade following the urban unrest chronicled in the Kerner Report. First, all three neighborhoods lost population at a notably faster rate than the city as a whole: whereas Chicago lost one-fifth of its population,

Oakland lost close to one-third, Washington Park 44 percent, and Grand Boulevard one-half. Second, while the proportion of employed adults remained roughly constant at 55 percent in the entire city, it plummeted in these poor neighborhoods: a majority of adults there were gainfully employed in all three areas in 1950, but by 1980 only one in three worked in Washington Park and one in four in Oakland and Grand Boulevard. As a result, the economic gap between the city and the population of these ghetto neighborhoods grew wider. Family income rose rapidly, citywide, after 1970, but edged up much more slowly in these neighborhoods. Thus, the median family income in Grand Boulevard fell from 62 percent of the city average in 1950 to less than 37 percent in 1980; in Oakland, the drop was from 65 percent to a mere 29 percent over this thirty-year period. Finally, although the percentage of owner-occupied housing units rose in Chicago from 30 percent in 1950 to close to 40 percent in 1980, it fell from 7 percent to an all-time low of 4 percent, on average, in these three inner-city neighborhoods. At the same time, the gap in median values of owner-occupied housing widened rapidly, especially after 1970. In Grand Boulevard, the value of housing in 1950 was 97 percent of the city average; by 1980 it had plummeted to about half the city average.

We could document additional facets of this growing schism between the evolution of Chicago as a whole (not to mention its suburbs) and its inner-city communities, including the closing of production sites, the disappearance of small stores and retail outlets, the demise of banking and credit institutions, the degradation of public services, the failure of the public-school system, etc. In sum, there has been a movement from an institutional ghetto—which fully duplicates the structure and activities of the larger society, as portrayed by Drake and Cayton forty years ago in their classic *Black Metropolis*[8]—back to a physical ghetto, which is incapable of providing basic services, resources, and opportunities.

As we previously mentioned, Chicago's black inner city has experienced a significant outmigration of the nonpoor, which has contributed to an incredible growth in the proportion of the adult population that has been excluded from gainful employment in these three neighborhoods. Between 1950 and 1980, the number of managers, officials, proprietors, professionals, and technical workers decreased by 58 percent (from 5,270 to 2,225); the number of clerical and sales workers by 53 percent (from 11,081 to 5,164). At the same time, the ranks of craftsmen and foremen dwindled from 6,564 to 1,338, while those of operatives and laborers dropped by 86 percent (from 35,808 to 4,889), and the number of private household and service workers decreased by 79 percent (from 25,182 to a mere 5,203). Overall, there was an alarming decrease in the proportion of employed adults, from 52 percent in 1950 to a historic low 27 percent in 1980.

To recapitulate what we have learned from this brief overview of the evolution of three of Chicago's poorest inner-city areas: from 1950 to 1980 there has emerged a growing schism between these areas and the city as a whole; this schism is part of a long-term process whereby disadvantage and deterioration accumulate in those neighborhoods that are worse off to begin with; and this phenomenon clearly *accelerated after 1970.* We shall argue later that these changes, and especially the drastic reduction of employed workers, have made inner-city neighborhoods increasingly vulnerable to the detrimental effects of the broader restructuring of the nation's economy.

THE ECONOMY AND THE CRISIS OF THE INNER CITY

The crisis of the ghetto cannot be explained by simplistic one-factor theories, and certainly not by racism alone nor by the alleged permissiveness of welfare programs. But if one had to choose the single most potent factor behind the growing misery of the ghetto, it would have to be the momentous economic transformations that have *undermined the manufacturing base* of central-city economies. The shift to service-producing sectors, the accelerating relocation of plants to overseas sites or to the suburbs and Sun Belt states, and the growing automation of industrial processes have combined to deplete employment opportunities in manufacturing. Those very blue-collar jobs upon which poor minorities are most dependent for steady employment and economic sustenance have disappeared by the hundreds of thousands, leaving behind what is for them an economic wasteland.

According to a study by John Kasarda, between 1947 and 1972 the central cities of the thirty-three largest metropolitan areas (based on 1970 census figures) lost 880,000 jobs in manufacturing at the same time that their suburbs gained 2.5 million manufacturing jobs.[9] These same cities lost an additional 867,000 jobs in retail and wholesale trade while millions of such jobs were added to the economies of their suburban areas. This dramatic decline in the demand for unskilled or semiskilled labor in goods-producing industries has been greatest in the older central cities of the Northeast and North Central regions. Thus, the cities of New York, Chicago, Philadelphia, and Detroit (which accounted for more than a quarter of the nation's central-city poor in 1982) together lost over a million jobs in manufacturing, wholesale, and retail firms in the decade between 1967 and 1976 alone.[10] It is true that this spectacular drop in blue-collar employment in large central cities has been partly offset by the rapid growth of "knowledge-intensive" services such as accounting, advertising, brokering, consulting, finance, and law. For example, from 1953 to 1984, New York City compensated for a loss of 600,000 manufacturing jobs by adding almost 700,000 jobs in white-collar services; Philadelphia lost 280,000 manufacturing jobs but gained 178,000 jobs in these services; and St. Louis gained 51,000 such white-collar positions as opposed to a loss of 127,000 jobs in manufacturing.[11] But it must be emphasized that these new jobs are the kind that are least accessible to the urban poor, who seldom possess the educational credentials, social skills, and cultural capital required by such positions.

This transformation of the urban economy has thus resulted in massive job losses in the very industries in which urban minorities tend to be concentrated, and significant employment gains in those industries where they are least represented and least likely to be hired. This is especially true for black males. In 1970, for instance, nearly half (42 percent) of all black males employed in the ten largest central cities of the country held traditional blue-collar jobs—that is, occupations categorized as operatives, transport workers, and laborers. By comparison, just over a third (37 percent) of employed Hispanic males and about a fifth (22 percent) of employed white males held these same types of jobs. Thus, black males were disproportionately affected by the deindustrialization of central cities, while white males were somewhat shielded from these structural changes by their more diverse employment. While no definitive research has established a direct correlation between these structural changes in the economy and the soaring rates of inner-city joblessness and labor-market exclusion, everything converges to indicate that they have had devastating consequences upon the work experiences and the employment prospects of poor urban minorities.

If urban black workers have been hit hard by the industrial and occupational transformation of the major central cities, they have also been adversely affected by the cyclical *downturns* of the American economy, including the stagnation of real wages and the sharp increases in unemployment that accompanied recessions from the early 1970s on. As pointed out by economist Frank Levy, the stagflation ushered in by the 1973 oil price increase drove real wages down by 5 percent in two years. Although real wages had regained their 1973 levels by 1979, the subsequent downturn in the economy set off another cycle of inflation, high unemployment, and low productivity growth, resulting in a full decade of wage stagnation. It was only because the proportion of the total population in the labor force increased from 41 to 50 percent between 1970 and today—owing in large measure to the increased labor-force participation of women, lower birthrates, and the coming of age of the large baby boom cohorts—that GNP (gross national product) per capita continued to rise, even though GNP per worker was not increasing.[12]

Furthermore, it is well known that manufacturing industries, a major source of urban black employment, particularly in the North, are especially sensitive to a slack economy. In recent years they have had to absorb the combined shock of increased foreign competition, stagflation, and technological upgrading. This has translated into massive employment cutbacks, wage cuts, and periodic layoffs—notably in older, central-city plants. Moreover, nonunion employees, low-wage workers, and newly hired workers in those industries, among which blacks are disproportionately represented, are most adversely affected by a recession-prone economy. They are not only the first to be dismissed; they are also those least likely to receive severance pay, unemployment benefits, or to be recalled on the job—in short, least likely to maintain ties to the world of work and means of economic self-sufficiency. One of the consequences of these recent increases in big-city unemployment has been "a growing polarization in the income distribution of black men. Compared to 1969, the proportions of black men with income below $5,000 and above $25,000 have both grown. Thus black men at the top of the distribution were doing progressively better while blacks at the bottom—between a fifth and a quarter of all black men ages 25–55—were doing progressively worse."[13]

Finally, the economic problems of low-income blacks have been reinforced by recent demographic factors resulting in a "labor surplus environment." As Levy puts it: "During the decade, women of all ages sharply increased their labor force participation and the large baby-boom cohorts of the 1950's came of age. Between 1960 and 1970, the labor force (nationwide) had grown by 13 million persons. But between 1970 and 1980, the labor force grew by 24 million persons. Because of this growth, we can assume that employers could be particularly choosy about whom they hired. In 1983, more than half of all black household heads in central-city poverty areas had not finished high school, a particular disadvantage in this kind of job market."[14] Indeed, recent research by Daniel Lichter has shown that the decline of entry-level jobs in central cities has "hurt most those seeking their first jobs—young adults, particularly those who are black and facing job competition greatly magnified by the rapid black concentration of this age segment in the central cities. Being black, young and poorly educated appears to be a poor formula for employment success in the 1980s."[15]

JOBLESSNESS, THE EXODUS OF WORKING FAMILIES, AND THE CHANGING SOCIAL ORGANIZATION OF THE INNER CITY

What are the mechanisms that link increased joblessness and the rising exclusion of adults from gainful employment to the growing concentration and spread of persistent poverty?[16] As revealed in our survey of the trends in the country's ten largest central cities, and in Chicago in particular, poor inner-city neighborhoods have undergone a profound social transformation over the past two decades or so. This is reflected not only in their increasing rates of social dislocation but also in their changing class structure.

In the 1940s, 1950s, and even as late as the 1960s in some metropolises, lower-class, working-class, and middle-class black families all resided more or less in the same ghetto areas, if on different streets. Confined by restrictive covenants and limited by systematic, institutional discrimination in their choice of employment and housing, the black middle-class professionals of the 1940s and 1950s (doctors, lawyers, teachers, social workers, etc.) resided in the higher-income areas of the inner city and, like the burgeoning black petty bourgeoisie, serviced the ghetto community. In contrast, the black middle class of today largely lives and is employed outside the inner city and seldom interacts with ghetto residents. Moreover, their exodus from the poorest neighborhoods has been increasingly accompanied by a movement of stable working-class black families to less depressed areas in other parts of the city and in the suburbs. This has significantly altered the pattern of social life in the ghetto. In earlier decades, the black working and middle classes brought stability to the inner city: they invested their economic and social resources in it; they patronized its churches, stores, banks, and community organizations; they sent their children to its schools; they reinforced societal norms and values, and made it meaningful for lower-class blacks to envision the possibility of limited upward mobility.

Today's ghetto residents, however, represent almost exclusively the most disadvantaged and oppressed segments of the urban black population—including those families that have experienced long-term spells of poverty and/or welfare receipt, individuals who lack minimal training and skills and have suffered periods of recurrent and persistent unemployment, adults who have dropped out of the labor force altogether, and those who are routinely involved in the underground economy or resort to street crime as a means of survival. The term "ghetto underclass" is increasingly employed by scholars and political analysts to designate this heterogeneous grouping of households and individuals who inhabit the cores of the country's central cities. We prefer to use it, not to denote the population itself, but rather to suggest that a *fundamental social transformation has taken place in ghetto neighborhoods,* such that the groups or categories comprised under this term are collectively different from and much more socially isolated than those that lived in these neighborhoods in earlier years. By "socially isolated" we mean that they find themselves in a qualitatively different social and institutional environment, where the structure of social and economic relations make it increasingly unlikely that they will have access to those minimal resources and channels necessary for escaping poverty.

The significance of this social transformation of the inner city is perhaps best captured by the concepts of "concentration effects" and of "social buffer." The term *concentration effects* refers to the added constraints and severe restriction of opportunities associated with living in a neighborhood in which the population is overwhelmingly socially disadvantaged. These constraints and opportunities drastically limit access to jobs, good schools and other public services, decent and safe housing, and availability of marriageable partners. The notion of a *social buffer* refers to the presence of a critical mass of working- and middle-class families to absorb the shock or cushion the effect of uneven economic growth and periodic recession on inner-city neighborhoods.

Our basic thesis, then, is *not* that some sort of "ghetto culture" went unchecked as nonpoor families left ghetto areas (as in the "culture of poverty" argument that keeps being revived under ever-new guises), but that the outmigration of these families makes it much more difficult, if not downright impossible, to sustain such basic institutions in the inner city as churches, banks, stores, schools, recreational facilities, and neighborhood associations in the face of massive and prolonged joblessness. At the same time, the exodus of working families and the demise of these institutions cuts off access to a number of traditional avenues of mobility, which then significantly alters the social perception of opportunity. These changing perceptions in turn determine social strategies (with regard to schooling, job search, marriage, etc.), which tend to reproduce the very conditions that produced them in the first place. That is, when the objective probability of achieving a stable and socially rewarding life, symbolized by the presence of stable working- and middle-class families, falls below a certain threshold, high aspirations can no longer be maintained and individuals are more likely to try to "adjust" to a condition that appears unchangeable and inevitable. A circular, dialectical process is set in motion, whereby the adjustment of subjective hopes and expectations to actual chances reinforces the objective mechanisms leading to increased isolation of the underclass. Though it may be true that the presence of stable working families in the ghetto, including members of the black middle class, reinforces by example the salience of mainstream values regarding family life, work, and educational achievement, a far more important effect is the *institutional and economic stability* these families are able to provide their neighborhoods because of their greater economic, social, and cultural resources, especially during periods of recession that bring about sharp rises in joblessness in those poor urban areas.

CONCLUSION

One of the legacies of historic racial oppression and of continued class subordination in the United States is a massive and growing ghetto underclass, highly concentrated in the nation's largest central cities, that is especially sensitive to the ongoing restructuring of the American economy. Indeed, despite the Great Society programs of the 1960s and the sweeping antidiscrimination and affirmative-action legislation of the 1970s, this unique vulnerability of the urban minority poor to cyclical downturns and sectoral shifts in the national economy, especially since 1970, has produced sharp increases in joblessness, persistent poverty, and the related problems of single-parent households, welfare receipt, housing deterioration, educational failure, and crime. In short, it has been at the heart of the crisis of the ghetto. These effects are most clearly seen in the concentrated poverty areas of the inner city. The recent exodus of working families, together with the sharp rise in unemployment, distorted the social structure of these neighborhoods in ways that severely aggravate the impact of periodic recessions, wage stagnation, the explosion of low-wage employment, and the ongoing spatial and industrial changes of the American economy. The dwindling presence of middle- and working-class households in the ghetto makes it considerably more difficult for the remaining residents of these communities to sustain basic institutions, formal and informal, in the face of rampant and prolonged joblessness and ensuing economic hardships. And, as the basic institutions decline, the social organization of inner-city neighborhoods deteriorates, further depleting the resources and life-chances of those who remain mired in these blighted areas.

How are these problems being addressed? The major response among policymakers recently has been to call for workfare programs as the major (if not sole) component of welfare reform. There is a basic assumption, sometimes explicit and sometimes implicit, in both liberal and conservative quarters, that the increasing woes of the ghetto underclass stem from inadequate social values, from a lack of work ethic among the poor, including the view that welfare receipt has become more attractive than working for a living.[17] As of today, and despite the clamoring sounds of the workfare advocates, there is neither rigorous research nor data to support the view that sagging values—the supposed "culture of poverty" or "welfare culture"—are at the root of the crisis of the inner city.[18] Indeed, the argument that more and more inner-city residents willingly elect to go on welfare rather than seek work (including low-paying jobs) because the former is more lucrative is directly contradicted by the fact that the purchasing power of welfare plummeted during the very period when rates of social dislocation in the inner city swung up. As Sheldon Danziger and Peter Gottschalk have shown, contrary to what is often believed, the real dollar value of AFDC plus food stamps actually decreased by 22 percent from 1972 to 1984, due to the failure of states to peg benefit levels to inflation.[19]

This analysis leads us to contend that, far from being caused by a mysterious and sudden collapse of values and of the moral fabric of individuals, the accelerating social dislocations that plague large inner cities in this country are due to fundamental, long-term structural changes in social and economic organization that have profoundly altered the social fabric of poor communities. To emphasize workfare and individual-level intervention is to slight the broader forces: this approach deflects attention from the critical consequences of shifts in the national economy, as they are mediated by the transformed class structure of ghetto neighborhoods. Until these evolving relations between economic organization, industrial mix, class structure, and poverty concentration in the inner city are confronted head-on, policies designed to address the social woes of the ghetto may perhaps provide a quick fix, momentarily ease social tensions, and please shortsighted political constituencies, but they will inevitably fall far short of improving the lives of the nation's truly disadvantaged.

Part IV

CONCLUSIONS AND RECOMMENDATIONS

"It is time now to turn with all the purpose at our command to the major unfinished business of this nation. It is time to adopt strategies for action that will produce quick and visible progress. It is time to make good the promises of American democracy to all citizens—urban and rural, white and black, Spanish-surname, American Indian, and every minority group."

So said the Kerner Report twenty years ago. It is that time again. The clock has been stopped on racial and economic progress in America—and is being turned back. For the victims, the consequences of our failure to act are increasingly severe. But in a sense, we will all be victims if our nation continues to become a more separated, more unfair, and less stable society.

That is why we organized the 1988 Commission on the Cities and, together with the University of New Mexico Institute for Public Policy and the Johnson Foundation, convened a national conference on "The Kerner Report: Twenty Years Later."

Lynn A. Curtis, one of the participants in that conference, makes clear in Chapter 8, that what needs to be done is do-able, both financially and politically; he calls attention to many local initiatives that have been inspired and successful, and he exhorts America to retreat from the folly of its present course.

The final chapter, Chapter 9, is the report of the 1988 Commission on the Cities and the national conference, updating, in brief, the Kerner Report. It is the synthesis and summary of the findings and recommendations in the earlier chapters of this book. Chapter 9 shows why and how America must now "make good the promises."

CHAPTER 8

Thomas Jefferson, the Kerner Commission, and the Retreat of Folly

LYNN A. CURTIS

IN 1769, THOMAS JEFFERSON placed an ad in the *Virginia Gazette:*

> *Run away from the subscriber in Albemarle, a Mulatto slave called Sandy, about 35 years of age. . . . He is a shoemaker by trade, in which he uses his left hand principally, can do coarse carpenter's work. . . . In his conversation he swears much, and his behavior is artful and knavish. He took with him a white horse . . . of which it is expected he will endeavor to dispose; he also carried his shoemaker's tools, and will probably endeavor to get employment that way. Whoever conveys the said slave to me in Albemarle, shall have 40s. reward. . . .*

Thomas Jefferson limited Sandy's job opportunities; he did not allow training beyond shoemaking and "coarse" carpentry. As a "rational" man of the European Enlightenment, he chose to label Sandy's adaptations to his lack of economic opportunity "artful and knavish." As a white rule-maker, Jefferson defined as a crime Sandy's decision to express himself as a human being by seeking freedom.

One hundred years later, the United States fought a civil war over this folly. That was the first civil-rights revolution.

Created in the midst of the second civil-rights revolution, the 1968 Kerner Report may have been too optimistic in its worst prognosis, as we can see now, twenty years later. In its *State of Black America, 1988,* the National Urban League reports that 25 percent of all black households are affected by crime. Rates of drug use, crime, and violent death are dramatically higher among blacks and Hispanics than among whites. Forty percent of black children are raised in fatherless homes. Rates of teenage pregnancy, infant mortality, and youth unemployment mark the continued deterioration of the old ghettos—from which much of the minority middle class has already escaped. The status of inner cities as separate and unequal zones in American life has been reinforced beyond the Kerner Report's predictions.

Today, there is a hard core of the very poor in American inner cities, minorities who were bypassed by the educational and economic gains of the 1970s. Many analysts label this group the underclass, though they do not agree on who constitutes the underclass, or on how large it is.[1]

Many people, including myself, find the term *underclass* demeaning. But one can agree with most contemporary observers that the truly disadvantaged must be defined not only in terms of low income but also in terms of self-defeating behavior and values. Examples include a girl's searching for respect and womanhood by having a baby in her early teens, or a boy's searching for respect and manhood by being violent and carrying a handgun or knife. The use by social scientists of the 1980s of income, behavior, and values to define the "at-risk" group is consistent with the definitions of the 1960s and 1970s—such as those of Elliot Liebow in *Tally's Corner,* Joyce Ladner in *Tomorrow's Tomorrow,* and Lee Rainwater in *Behind Ghetto Walls.*

For example, Rainwater's summary statement of 1970 is consistent with the Kerner Report findings, and holds up very well today:

White cupidity
creates

structural conditions highly inimical to basic social
adaptation (low income availability, poor education,
poor services, stigmatization)

to which Blacks adapt
by

social and personal responses which serve to sustain
the individual in his punishing world
but also to generate aggressiveness
toward the self and others

which results in

suffering directly inflicted by Blacks on themselves
and on others

THE RETREAT OF FOLLY: AN ILLUSTRATION

In terms of federal policy toward the inner city since the Kerner Report, Barbara Tuchman's analysis of folly continues to be relevant:

> *Folly is the pursuit by governments of policies contrary to their own interests. . . . In its first stage, mental standstill fixes on the principles and boundaries governing a political problem. In the second stage, when dissonances and failing function begin to appear, the initial principles rigidify. . . . Rigidifying leads to increase of investment and the need to protect egos; policy founded upon error multiplies, never retreats . . . until it causes . . . the fall of Troy . . . [*or*] the classic humiliation in Vietnam.*

The presidential commissions of the late 1960s prompted the government to "throw money at the problems" without getting enough sound advice on how to implement specific programs on the mean streets. The folly was to throw more and more money at the problems, apparently with inadequate results. Nonetheless we have experienced practical, if isolated, grass-roots successes over the last twenty years.

We must build on these local, indigenous successes if we are to force the folly of federal policy to retreat. We need to acknowledge the racism of Jefferson and the misdirection of "top-down" solutions through which, in Tuchman's words, egos are protected by the multiplication of policy errors. The key is to empower the contemporary Sandys—those who live in the Robert Taylor Homes or in the South Bronx, and even in Liberty City (perhaps the most intractable of all places)—to experiment, to create, to "bubble up" a new federal policy.

An example of what can, and what cannot, be done locally may clarify what it means to "bubble up" federal policy.

A few months ago, the *Washington Post* described how, in a "clean-sweep" operation, the police tried to push drug dealers out of a certain local street. The dealers had been employing very young women to sit on doorsteps with walkie-talkies and tell the dealers when the police were near.

The police action cleared the street, but it merely displaced the problem to another street. It did nothing about the fact that the women were single teenage mothers who had dropped out of school. The mothers needed the money—or they needed programs such as those supported by philanthropist Irving Harris at Chicago's Beethoven housing project, to provide a fair head start for their kids, so that the children might find occupations other than pushing and stealing. Many of the Washington drug dealers themselves were single fathers. Based on existing evidence, some of the fathers, and mothers, could have benefited from Eugene Lang's I Have a Dream program in New York to motivate students to finish high school by offering college financing—and long-term guidance. Others could no doubt benefit from the kind of computer-based training that Robert Taggert has demonstrated to be a highly cost-effective form of remedial education, leading to solid, legal labor-market employment. Such training of young fathers might be matched with an offer of employment on the condition that some of the earnings be transferred to support their infants.

Perhaps the employer could be a community organization that rehabilitates and weatherizes houses in the same neighborhood. This could provide shelter for the homeless, as well as new facilities for programs in teen parenting, school-dropout prevention, job training, and crime prevention.

Such economic development of the neighborhood might create a demand for more employment of high-risk youth. It might empower the neighborhood-based development corporation to apply for a foundation or government grant to better establish the rehabilitation enterprise and make it financially self-sustaining.

As with the community-based Around the Corner to the World program in Washington, D.C., the high-risk youth working in the business might form peer support groups to help one another when times are rough and when competing, illegal labor-market opportunities become tempting. (We have learned over the last twenty years that social support services are crucial for making employment programs for the disadvantaged work.) The employees in the business could serve as big brothers or big sisters to the neighborhood kids, who might otherwise turn to drugs, crime, and adolescent pregnancy.

The police could help by team-policing on foot patrols, realistically understood not as a way to reduce crime (there is little proof that they can), but as a stabilizing influence in the neighborhood that would make it easier for others to pursue economic development and address the *causes* of crime. Off-duty police could help youth with job training. That is what Anthony Bouza, now police chief of Minneapolis, authorized for some of his officers when he was a captain in the Bronx. Law enforcement might follow the lead of police in Ponce, Puerto Rico, and refer high-risk kids to the house-weatherization business, where staff could serve as advocates—mediators between the youth and the criminal-justice system.

The dilemmas of teenage pregnancy, crime, drugs, dropping out, and unemployment are interrelated: they cause and affect one another. Government statistics now show that the two societies foreseen by the Kerner Report are even more separate and less equal than in 1968. But the purpose of the foregoing scenario—parable, if you will—is to show that there can be similarly interrelated solutions at the grass-roots level.

Indigenous inner-city organizations have in fact created such solutions since 1968. The common principles that appear to underlie their success involve the need to create, through peer support and mentors, an extended-family setting with strict rules and nurturing—through which self-respect is instilled, community-based education is pursued, job training is undertaken, and local employment is found by youths who are at high risk of dropping out of high school, becoming jobless, committing crime, or becoming teenage parents.

In the process of turning around high-risk youth through these principles, self-esteem is *the* key—the sine qua non for such goals as staying in school. Whether to effectively deter thirteen-year-olds from having babies or sixteen-years-olds from robbing, improved self-esteem is perhaps the most salient instrument of change among minority youth that is consistent with the priorities of the Kerner Report.

The best available evaluation evidence and cost-benefit studies since the late sixties point to programs like the Argus Community in the South Bronx, Centro Sister Isolina Ferre in Ponce, Puerto Rico, and the House of Umoja in West Philadelphia as good examples of first-generation successes with these underlying principles.[2] These programs have done for indigenous social development what inner-city organizations like the Bedford-Stuyvesant Restoration Corporation in New York, the Woodlawn Organization in Chicago, and TELECU in Los Angeles have done for indigenous economic development.

THE CORNERSTONE OF NEW NATIONAL POLICY: MECHANISMS FOR LOCAL EMPOWERMENT

These and other inner-city organizations understand that real communities thrive or fail to thrive, and become healthy or pathological, mainly as a result of the strength or weakness of basic institutions—work, family and kin, religious and communal associations, and a vibrant local economy capable of generating stable livelihoods.

In turn, the objective of a national private- and public-sector policy, consistent with the Kerner Report and focused on the inner city, is to replicate widely the principles underlying these successes—and to create the national financial mechanisms that will sustain the replications.

As one might extrapolate from Neal Peirce and Carol Steinbach's Ford Foundation report *Corrective Capitalism: The Rise of America's Community Development Corporations*, a policy that steadily expands and strengthens minority-controlled inner-city organizations can eventually have a major national impact—*if* enough resources are pumped to the grass-roots levels.

In the 1970s and 1980s, new private-sector national "intermediate institutions" have been created. Examples are the Local Initiatives Support Corporation, the Enterprise Foundation, Public/Private Ventures, and the Eisenhower Foundation. These institutions aim to expand the number of competent inner-city organizations that can generate social and economic development. Related national organizations, like the Development Training Institute and the Center for

Community Change, provide management training and technical assistance to the leaders of community-based organizations.

Public-sector institutions should consider utilizing private intermediate institutions more, for administration, technical assistance, and evaluation of at least some new initiatives—on the grounds that the existing private institutions appear to be more cost-effective than the public ones, and that the intermediaries could then directly fund community-based organizations.

The federal agencies most responsible for policies advocated by the Kerner Report—Labor, Health and Human Services, Education, and Justice—could often take on the role of funders and monitors of the more efficient private-sector intermediaries, which, in turn, could arrange private-sector matches. The intermediaries would support and expand community-based organizations that would generate social and economic reconstruction within specific inner-city neighborhoods. The federal government could continue to administer successful programs, like Job Corps and Head Start.

FEDERAL POLICY: THE REST OF THE PICTURE

This is not the place to detail a new national inner-city urban policy, but a few major points can be made. Beyond the cornerstone of grass-roots inner-city organization empowerment, the nation's experience since the Kerner Commission suggests that a new federal policy also needs to:

... Follow the recommendations of the Committee for Economic Development on significantly expanding early-childhood development initiatives that build on Head Start and Project Beethoven.

... Replicate successesful programs to revitalize inner-city schools, like the one in Minneapolis formerly headed by Richard Green, now school chancellor in New York City.

... Call on someone like Robert Taggert to draft federal legislation to implement a job-training program based on his successful computer-based remediation and training programs, as well as on the experience of the Manpower Demonstration Research Corporation.

... Reform the national welfare system by building on evaluations of the innovations in Wisconsin known collectively as the Child Support Assurance System, and the ET program in Massachusetts.

... Expand programs for new housing and economic development, and target them better to the inner city, with the goal of generating jobs in the ghetto while rehabilitating its infrastructure.

... Reform "trickle-down" economic development programs and proposals—like Urban Development Action Grants and Urban Enterprise Zones—so that they are undertaken through minority, nonprofit, inner-city development corporations rather than through corporate contractors.

... Listen to the (business-oriented) National Association of Manufacturers when it defends the executive order under which many federal contractors set numerical goals for hiring blacks, Hispanics, and women.

- Encourage proactive community-oriented policing, like that in Japan, rather than the reactive operations (only after a crime) that now predominate in the United States.

- Better understand that there are scale economies in integrating inner-city economic and infrastructure development, on the one hand, and employment and social-support services, on the other.

- Recognize that, based on repeated experience, the best way to avoid inevitable cabinet-level infighting on a coordinated federal inner-city policy is to place the coordinating lead in the White House, not in an agency.

FINANCING AND MACROECONOMIC POLICY

A few months ago in the Sunday *New York Times,* Daniel Patrick Moynihan, as he is wont to do, quoted a French theologian: "The worst, most corrupting lies are problems poorly stated."

In 1981 an American Enterprise Institute conference on domestic policy stated much of the problem in terms of insufficient volunteerism. Most community leaders at the conference stated the problem in terms of lack of money. Today, even the hard-nosed CEOs on the Committee for Economic Development, in their *Children in Need* report on

Beethoven-project-type preschool education, talk about significant new spending targeted at programs that have proven themselves. Ernest Boyer, president of the Carnegie Endowment for Teaching, reminds us that, even at a national level, such programs, especially for the inner-city poor, would cost less than two aircraft carriers.

The point is that we cannot fall into the well-laid trap that says the American budget and trade deficits prevent new inner-city spending.

In fact, there are an almost infinite number of creative fiduciary solutions. All we really need to do is change our priorities. A 1 percent increase in employment reduces the federal deficit by $30 billion. New gasoline taxes could raise $100 billion—and still leave gas prices lower than in Europe. *Business Week* has put the cost of expanding (nonresidential) programs in remediation, job training, life skills, and family support to reach everyone who needs them (3.5 million people, minority and white) at about $13 billion per year. The *Business Week* estimate is considerably higher than the $3 billion currently spent on job training and employment, but it also is considerably less than the $20 billion per year currently spent on welfare programs.

Whatever definition of the truly disadvantaged one accepts, it should be kept in mind that the numbers are not overwhelming. We are talking about between 2 million and somewhat over 10 million persons. A new national policy is manageable with numbers in this range. Just consider the percentages of federal spending for defense versus other programs. The 41 percent of the budget currently allocated to defense is up from 35 percent in 1980. Today, 1 percent is spent on education (down from 2 percent in 1980), and less than 1 percent is spent on training and employment programs. This is a minuscule part of the total. Even if we doubled the percentages of the budget allocated to education, job training, and community development, the amount would only roughly equal the increase in the military budget since 1980. One implication is that, compared to the federal defense budget, relatively modest increases in federal domestic spending, if properly targeted, can make a significant difference.

The macroeconomic policy that must accompany increased domestic spending has been outlined by Robert Kuttner:

> *The worst national leadership could do in the present circumstances would be to embrace the economics of austerity and the politics of fiscal impotence. Taxes should indeed be raised—on those who can afford to pay—but they should be spent, partly on deficit reduction and substantially on the public needs that have gone untended. Real Keynesianism—an economics of stabilization, public spending, low interest rates and high growth—should be taken off the shelf and wielded.* [3]

As part of the overall economic direction, federal resources must be aimed directly at the community level because, as Harvard's Richard Neustadt and Ernest May point out in *Thinking in Time,* trickle-down benefits from economic growth, despite ebullient can-do American political rhetoric, have never solved the real problems of the disadvantaged.

However, the "rising tide" philosophy—to lift *all* ships—is relevant in that we need a broad economic framework that ensures sufficient job opportunity. This means the kind of demand-side economic policy of the early 1960s that produced 4 percent unemployment and low inflation. It does not mean the supply-side economics of the 1980s, which have fostered further division of America into two societies—one rich and prospering and one poor and becoming poorer.

As Neustadt and May remind us, Americans are notoriously lacking in historical perspective. At this point in our history, such perspective can be used to reinforce the argument for increased domestic spending. In *The Rise and Fall of the Great Powers,* Yale historian Paul Kennedy has convincingly shown how over the last five hundred years the more nations increase their power, the larger proportion of their resources are devoted to maintaining it. If too large a proportion of resources is diverted to military purposes, national power weakens in the long run and there is internal decay. This has happened to Spain, the Netherlands, France, England, the Soviet Union, and, today, the United States. We have fallen behind as a nation.

- Functional illiteracy is an astounding 20 percent in the United States, compared to less than 1 percent in Japan, which has a much more difficult written language.

- The American crime rate remains by far the highest in the industrialized world.

- Our economic growth rate lags behind our chief Western rivals.

- All informed economists agree that our industrial infrastructure has significantly eroded.

Paul Kennedy concludes that we require a more reasonable balance between military and nonmilitary expenditure. There is a particular need for nonmilitary research and development, including, let us emphasize, the social and economic development required to reverse the increasing devastation of our inner cities.

POLITICAL FEASIBILITY

In resurrecting the recommendations of the Kerner Report, drawing on the wisdom gained over the last twenty years, we need the kind of leadership that President Kennedy showed when he called for a ten-year plan to land a man on the moon—a goal he set in motion knowing that it would have to be continued by other administrations.

A creative national leader can use public opinion to forge a new industrial policy along the lines proposed by Gar Alperovitz, Jeff Faux, Barry Bluestone, and Bennett Harrison—and ensure in the process that the policy significantly benefits the truly disadvantaged and the inner city.

For example, in a World Policy Institute poll, wide majorities of Americans have said that while military power has grown, the American economy has gotten "weaker relative to other countries" and America's industries are "not geared to keeping up with the changes taking place in the world economy." Protests by white members of Congress about embracing the poor within an industrial policy can be countered by a presidential adviser who points out that more of the poor are white than black.

National leadership should also remember that in the 1980s a conservative president has praised the House of Umoja before the National Alliance of Business, saying that Umoja has done "what all the police and social welfare agencies have failed to do." Similarly, the Argus Community has been praised in the *Wall Street Journal* as "an inner city school that works." Advocates from the 1960s who sought "community action" and sponsored "mobilization for youth" came from a different philosophic position than the observers who today want people to "pull themselves up by their bootstraps." Yet there is some political common ground here, a certain shared support of "self-help" by progressives and conservatives, and it can be built upon.

A sound political strategy can be a moral one, too. As Michael Sandel has argued in the *New Republic,* a "public life empty of moral meanings and shared ideals does not secure freedom but offers an open invitation to intolerance."[4] We are at a moral disadvantage in the eyes of the world, and especially the Third World, when Raisa Gorbachev asks about our poverty and homelessness during a trip to Washington, D.C. The fundamental message of the Kerner Report is a moral one.

Historically, the nation has veered between public action and private interest. Ralph Waldo Emerson observed that both led to excess over time, though we also can reasonably conclude from American history that periods of uncontrolled private interest generally are holding actions, whereas democratic reforms produce enduring change.

At the end of this recent period of retrenchment, history should remind us that neglected problems become acute and demand remedy. People grow weary of materialism as their ultimate goal. They ask not what their country can do for them but what they can do for their country. With the cycles of the twentieth century as a guide, Arthur Schlesinger predicts that at "some point, shortly before or after the year 1990," the nation will return to reform, comparable to that at the turn of the century, in the 1930s, and in the 1960s.

And we have learned, over the last twenty years, much about the day-to-day, nitty-gritty process of street-level implementation—something of which most policymakers and legislators within the Washington Beltway are oblivious.

If we finally show the political courage to empower the poor, folly can be forced to retreat, and the agenda of the Kerner Commission can be completed.

CHAPTER 9

Race and Poverty in the United States—and What Should Be Done

1988 COMMISSION ON THE CITIES

FOR A TIME following the Kerner Report—from the late 1960s through the mid-1970s—America made progress on all fronts. Then came a series of severe economic shocks that hit the most vulnerable people hardest. Poverty is worse now for black Americans, Hispanic Americans, American Indians, and other minorities. But not just for them. The rise in unemployment and poverty has cut across racial and ethnic lines—and affects both minorities and whites. (More whites than minority people are poor.)

POVERTY IS WORSE AND MORE PERSISTENT

From the late 1960s through the 1980s, a series of recessions—most often precipitated or accentuated by a restrictive monetary policy and high interest rates—culminated in an economic crisis as bad as any since the 1930s.

The closing of many urban manufacturing plants and the removal of blue-collar jobs to the suburbs, as well as the loss of blue-collar jobs altogether—trends the Kerner Report had called attention to—accelerated. These were the very jobs upon which central-city residents had been most dependent.

The rise and fall of the unemployment rates through the last twenty years have been closely tied to poverty rates.

Fast-food and other retail service jobs replaced some of this lost employment, but at much lower pay. The higher-pay new service jobs that came to the cities—in accounting, finance, the professions, and the like—were those least available to the workers left in the inner cities.

Efforts to break unions were successful. Wage "give-backs" were common. The federal minimum wage, which had been raised four times between 1978 and 1981 (during which time employment rose 9 percent), was not raised again after 1981.

Poverty increased. Census figures show that in 1986, 32.4 million Americans were poor (compared with 24.1 million in 1969). This included about 22 million whites, nearly 9 million blacks, and about 5 million Hispanics.

In 1986, according to the census, 2 million Americans were poor—even though they were working full-time and year-round—52 percent more than in 1975, and 22 percent more than in 1980. Another 6.9 million people were working part-time, or full-time for a part of the year, and still could not earn enough to get above the poverty line.

From 1980 through June 1987, average weekly earnings increased from $235 to $305, but adjusted for inflation, this represented, in fact, a *drop* in real wages—down to $227. (This was true even though productivity had risen at an impressive average of 4 percent a year from 1981 to 1985, and had increased in 1986 by 3.5 percent—better than either Japan or Germany.)

Nearly 6 percent of Americans—nearly 8 million people—are officially unemployed. They are actively searching for work without success. Another 1 million "discouraged" workers have given up and stopped looking for jobs.

Cuts in Social Programs

Political efforts to cut federal education, housing, job-training, and other social programs became more determined. These efforts were largely successful.

Today, less than 1 percent of the federal budget is spent for education, down from 2 percent in 1980. Job training and job subsidization programs were cut nearly 70 percent—from $9 billion in 1981 to only $4 billion.

Less than 1 percent of the federal budget is now spent on training and job programs. Yet that part of the federal budget spent on the military has increased from 35 percent in 1980 to 41 percent today.

Job-training funds peaked in 1978. Not only have they gone down since then, but the declining funds are now mainly used for the least disadvantaged, leaving very little for high-school dropouts and the less skilled.

A quarter of a million young people—25 percent of the total when President Reagan took office—have been cut from the Summer Youth Employment Program.

Federal spending for non-insurance social programs, as a percentage of Gross National Product, has gone down from 4.2 percent in 1980 to 3.7 percent last year, while defense expenditures have increased during the same period from 5.2 percent to 6.9 percent.

With inflation, the real income of welfare recipients has been reduced nationally by approximately one-third since 1970; in Chicago, for example, the value of AFDC (Aid to Families with Dependent Children) has been halved during that time.

Poverty Worsened and Deepened

The gap between the rich and poor has widened. In 1986 the top one-fifth of American households received 46.1 percent of total income, up from 43.3 percent in 1970; the income share of the middle three-fifths declined from 52.7 percent to 50.2 percent; and that of the poorest one-fifth of households went down from 4.1 percent to 3.8 percent.

Census figures also show that poverty has become more prevalent in America's central cities. There the poverty rates rose by half from 1969 to 1985—increasing from 12.7 percent to 19 percent, a much steeper rise than for those outside.

Poverty has deepened. Typically, poor people living in big cities in the 1980s are farther below the poverty line than their counterparts of the 1960s. There was a sharp increase between 1970 and 1982 in the percentage of poor people with incomes more than 25 percent below the poverty line.

Urban poverty has become more persistent. According

to Professor Greg J. Duncan of the University of Michigan's Survey Research Center, "The chances a poor person in a highly urbanized county would escape his poverty have fallen substantially since the 1970s," after some improvement between the late 1960s and mid-1970s, and are now well below the levels of twenty years ago.

"The increased persistence of urban poverty is alarming," Professor Duncan says. "Persistently inadequate living standards not only make life miserable for the families involved, but also reduce the chances that children will succeed in school and jobs when they grow up."

A GROWING AMERICAN "UNDERCLASS"

Blacks and other minorities have made important progress, legally and politically. The black middle class has grown. In 1965 there were only 200 black elected officials; by 1986 that figure had mushroomed to 6,500. Blacks and other minorities have made significant inroads in the media, law enforcement, business, and the professions. But progress has slowed, and the Reagan administration has tried to turn the clock back.

Lack of Vigorous Affirmative Action

Though the Supreme Court has several times recently upheld affirmative action in hiring and promotions, the Reagan administration has been hostile to affirmative-action efforts and to the vigorous enforcement of civil-rights laws.

Ralph G. Neas, executive director of the Leadership Conference on Civil Rights, has declared: "EEOC [Equal Employment Opportunity Commission] has become less vigorous in enforcing the law and has abandoned many of the civil rights remedies employed by previous Republican and Democratic administrations."

Cutbacks in affirmative-action enforcement have been unfortunate, especially because earlier efforts had been successful in increasing jobs and influence for blacks and in recruiting more blacks into higher education. Affirmative action worked.

Incentives for integrated housing have been ended by the Reagan administration, incentives for subsidized housing have all but been eliminated, and civil-rights enforcement in the Community Development Block Grant program has stopped.

The Kerner Commission recommended an open housing law. But the Fair Housing Law actually adopted in 1968 proved to be too weak and without adequate enforcement machinery. All the secretaries of HUD recommended strengthening it; but it was not until 1988 that Congress passed a stronger law.

More "Separate Societies"

The Kerner Report warning is coming true: America *is* again becoming two separate societies, one black (and, today, we can add to that, Hispanic) and one white—separate and unequal.

While there are few all-white neighborhoods, and there

is some integration even in black neighborhoods, segregation by race still sharply divides America's cities—in both housing and schools for blacks, and especially in schools for Hispanics. This is true despite increases in suburbanization and the numbers of blacks and other minorities who have entered the middle class.

For the big cities studied by the Kerner Commission, housing segregation has changed little, if any, and is worse in terms of housing costs for blacks, who are more likely than whites to be renters. Segregation is not just a matter of income; it still cuts across income and education levels. Studies show continued discrimination in housing sales and rentals and in mortgage financing for blacks and Hispanics.

Segregation breeds further inequality for blacks and other minorities—including lessened opportunities for work and the greater likelihood of inferior education.

Segregated housing produces segregated schools, and most often this means worse schools for blacks and Hispanics than those available to whites.

From 1968 to 1984, the number of white students in the public schools dropped by 19 percent, while the number of black students increased by 2 percent. Hispanic student numbers skyrocketed, up 80 percent.

Public schools are becoming more segregated. There has been no national school desegregation progress since the last favorable Supreme Court decision in this field in 1972. After declining from 1968 to 1976, the number of black students enrolled in predominantly minority schools increased, from 62.9 percent in 1980 to 63.5 percent in 1984. The percentage of Hispanic students enrolled in minority schools has climbed steadily from 54.8 percent to 70.6 percent during the same period.

University of Chicago political scientist Gary Orfield has

found that "a great many black students, and very rapidly growing numbers of Hispanic students, are trapped in schools where more than half of the students drop out, where the average achievement level of those who remain is so low that there is little serious pre-collegiate instruction, where pre-collegiate courses and counselors are much less available, and which only prepare students for the least competitive colleges." There have been severe cuts in federal student-assistance funds.

The American Council on Education has said that the gap between black and white college-going rates is larger now than it has been in more than a quarter of a century.

The high-school graduation rate for black students rose to 75.6 percent in 1985, but the percentage of these students going on to college has been declining since 1976, dropping to 26.1 percent in 1985. Similarly, the high-school graduation rate for Hispanic students was 62.5 percent in 1985, but the percentage who enrolled in college had been on a four-year decline by that year and fell to to only 26.9 percent in 1985. The college-going rate for American Indian students is also on the decline.

Greater Racial Contrast

Nonwhite unemployment in 1968 was 6.7 percent, compared to 3.2 percent for whites. Today, overall employment has doubled, and black unemployment is more than double white unemployment.

Median black family income, as a percentage of median white family income, dropped from 60 percent in 1968 to 57.1 percent in 1986. Those who would be classified as "working poor" if they were white—those with annual incomes between $9,941 and $18,700—are the middle class for black families; that is the present range of median black family income.

From these facts of black and Hispanic segregation and inequality, Professor Orfield has concluded that the ghettos and barrios of America's cities are "separate and deteriorating societies, with separate economies, increasingly divergent family structures and basic institutions, and even growing linguistic separation. The physical separation by race, class, and economic situation is much greater than it was in the 1960s, the level of impoverishment, joblessness, educational inequality, and housing even more severe."

The Urban Underclass

The result of these trends is a persistent, large, and growing American urban underclass.

Poverty is both urban and rural, both white and minority. But the great majority of the nation's poor people—70.4 percent in 1985—live in metropolitan areas. From 1974 to 1983, over 33 percent of highly urban population (those living in the nation's 56 most highly urban counties) were poor at least once, and 5.2 percent were poor at least 80 percent of the time. During the same period, 60 percent of blacks in these areas were poor at least once, and 21.1 percent were poor at least 80 percent of the time.

Central-city poverty has become more concentrated. From 1974 to 1985, in central-city poverty tracts with a poverty rate of 20 percent or more, the numbers of people living in poverty nearly doubled—from 4.1 million to 7.8 million. In areas of extreme poverty—more than 40 percent—the numbers of white families living in poverty went up 44 percent, the numbers of black families 104 percent, and the numbers of Hispanic families 300 percent.

University of Chicago sociologist William Julius Wilson has found a resulting "rapid social deterioration" in the inner-city neighborhoods since the Kerner Report, with "sharp increases in social dislocation and the massive breakdown of social institutions in ghetto areas."

Concentrated poverty is "one of the legacies of racial and class oppression," Professor Wilson has stated, and it has produced what he has termed "concentration effects"—the "added constraints and severe restrictions of opportunities associated with living in a neighborhood in which the population is overwhelmingly socially disadvantaged—constraints and opportunities with regard to access to jobs, good schools and other public services, and availability of marriageable partners." The result in these concentrated, central-city areas, he has said, is "sharp increases in joblessness, poverty, and the related problems of single-parent households, welfare dependency, housing deterioration, educational failure, and crime."

NATIONAL SECURITY REQUIRES NEW HUMAN INVESTMENT

"Quiet riots" are taking place in America's major cities: unemployment, poverty, social disorganization, segregation, family disintegration, housing and school deterioration, and crime.

These "quiet riots" may not be as alarming or as noticeable to outsiders—unless they are among the high proportion of Americans who are victimized by crime—but they are even more destructive of human life than the violent riots of twenty years ago.

This destruction of our human capital is a serious threat to America's national security. The Kerner Report said: "It is time to make good the promises of American democracy to all citizens—urban and rural, white and black, Spanish-surname, American Indian, and every minority group."

A recommitment now to that kind of human investment could begin to move us once again toward becoming a more stable and secure society of self-esteem.

As Roger W. Wilkins, a former assistant attorney general and now Clarence Robinson Professor of History at George Mason University, has said, "The problem is not a problem of defective people; the problem is a problem of a defective system."

The resistance of the system to change, its inflexibility, is nowhere better illustrated than in the failure of the federal government to fully implement Indian tribal self-determination and self-government; there has been little visible effect from two initiatives toward that end—a presidential one in 1968 and a congressional one in 1975.

We know what should be done.

Jobs. Jobs are the greatest need. Full employment is the best anti-poverty program. An economic policy of stabilization, greater spending for targeted social programs, low interest rates, and greater growth is essential. (A decline of 1 percent in unemployment could reduce the federal deficit by $30 billion.)

We need a strong public jobs program; there is plenty of infrastructure work that needs to be done. The minimum wage must be raised. The tax laws should be changed further to see that the working poor get to keep more of their earnings. Increased training for jobs must be provided, along with a sound national day-care program for mothers who want to work.

Welfare. We should provide better income for those who are unable to work or cannot find work. There should be national standards for AFDC.

Desegregation. A stronger fair-housing law has finally been passed; it, and other affirmative action laws, should be vigorously enforced. More large-scale desegregation of schools is needed; where such actions have been tried, they have worked and produced stability over long periods of time. A majority of Americans under thirty, as well as a majority of college students as a group, support such desegregation. So do two-thirds of the families whose children have actually been bussed for desegregation purposes.

Affirmative action. Vigorous enforcement of equal-employment opportunity and affirmative-action laws is vital. Where public funds or subsidies are used, there must be strict requirements for affirmative action and contract compliance.

Health. We need to extend national health insurance to more Americans, including the requirement of health insurance as a part of job benefits. This is important if we are to change our present two-tiered system, composed of those covered by health insurance and those who are not.

General. Childhood development is fundamentally important; we know that programs like Head Start work, and they now are advocated by corporate leaders like those on the Committee for Economic Development. The Job Corps works, too. We should give these programs added support. We should replicate successes in inner-city schools like those in Minneapolis.

These things are do-able. And we have the means. Doubling the percentage of the federal budget that now goes for job training, education, and community development, for example, would still only roughly match the percentage increase in military spending since 1980.

The numbers of people in the underclass are relatively small. Improving their chances and their lives is increasingly in the self-interest of whites as whites become a declining proportion of America's population. Further, the fact that the labor force is shrinking as a percentage of total population should be seen as an increasing opportunity for finding work for the chronically unemployed.

We must find the will. A majority of Americans support increased spending for social programs (and believe that the military budget is the best place for cuts). They support the idea that more should be done to give a hand to black people and other minorities.

The problem is that, because we made progress for a time, most Americans—as well as American policymakers—think that we are still making progress or that most inequalities have disappeared. This is not true.

We must bring the problems of race, unemployment, and poverty back into the public consciousness, put them back on the public agenda.

That is our purpose in making this new report.

Notes and Sources

CHAPTER 1: THE 1967 RIOTS AND THE KERNER COMMISSION BY FRED R. HARRIS

Notes

1. Information on black poverty and black-white disorders in the 1960s and earlier is taken from Fred R. Harris, *Alarms and Hopes* (New York: Harper and Row, 1968).

2. Rick Lyman, "The Unlearned Lessons of America's Racial Riots," *Philadelphia Inquirer,* July 19, 1987.

3. John Bussey, "Detroit's Racial Woes Persist Two Decades after Devastating Riot," *Wall Street Journal,* June 17, 1987; and Bill Peterson,

"Twenty Years after Riots, Inequalities Still Burden Detroit's Blacks," *Washington Post,* July 28, 1987.

CHAPTER 3: POVERTY IS STILL WITH US—AND WORSE BY DAVID HAMILTON

Notes

1. *Albuquerque Journal,* February 10, 1988.
2. Bettman, *The Good Old Days,* p. xi.
3. George, *Progress and Poverty,* p. 7.
4. Shannon, *The Great Depression,* especially pp. 13–14.
5. Riesman, *The Lonely Crowd;* Krutch, *Human Nature.*
6. Harrington, *The Other America;* Kolko, *Wealth and Power;* Morgan et al., *Income and Welfare.* Interestingly, these works seemed to set off a veritable flood of publications on the matter of poverty. By 1969 the flood diminished rather quickly, and by 1972 the flow was reduced to a trickle. Thus it has always been on the rediscovery of poverty. All kinds of instant experts arrive, and just as suddenly move on once the research money disappears.
7. Gilder, *Wealth and Poverty.*
8. Trattner, *History of Social Welfare;* Patterson, *Struggle against Poverty.*
9. *Economic Report of the President, 1964,* p. 59.
10. *Ibid.,* p. 77.
11. Nourse, *America's Capacity to Produce,* chapter 20.
12. Leven et al., *America's Capacity to Consume.*
13. Rogers, *Poor Women, Poor Families,* chapter 2.
14. Harrington, *The New American Poverty,* p. 229.
15. Goldschmidt, *Comparative Functionalism.*
16. Goldschmidt, *Man's Way,* chapter 3; Ayres, *Theory of Economic Progress,* chapters 5, 8, and 9. Goldschmidt treats the matter of status and role from the standpoint of the anthropologist; Ayres does so in the application to economics. See also Hamilton, "Political Economy of Poverty," for the application of this analysis to the problem of poverty.
17. Wootton, *Social Foundations of British Wage Policy.*

18. Holman, *Poverty,* chapter 5.

19. Ryan, *Blaming the Victim.*

20. There is a steady outpouring of works from the purported think tanks of the conservatives that dilate on the evils of doing anything about the plight of the poor: the best of intentions lead inevitably to unexpected consequences, say Irving Kristol and his ilk. It is a recipe for laissez-faire and the status quo. It is very reminiscent of the atmosphere a century and a half ago in England: Parliament repealed the Poor Laws and called it reform.

21. *Economic Report of the President, 1964,* p. 78.

Sources

Ayres, C. E. *The Theory of Economic Progress.* Chapel Hill: University of North Carolina Press, 1944.

Bettman, Otto J. *The Good Old Days—They Were Terrible.* New York: Random House, 1974.

Economic Report of the President, 1964. Washington, D.C.: Government Printing Office, 1964.

George, Henry. *Progress and Poverty.* New York: Random House, Modern Library, 1938.

Gilder, George. *Wealth and Poverty.* New York: Bantam, 1982.

Goldschmidt, Walter. *Comparative Functionalism.* Berkeley: University of California Press, 1966.

———. *Man's Way.* New York: Holt, 1959.

Hamilton, David. "The Political Economy of Poverty: Institutional and Technological Dimensions." *Journal of Economic Issues,* vol. 1, no. 4 (December 1967), pp. 309–320.

Harrington, Michael. *The New American Poverty.* New York: Penguin, 1984.

———. *The Other America.* New York: Macmillan, 1962.

Holman, Robert. *Poverty: Explanations of Social Deprivation.* New York: St. Martin's, 1978.

Kolko, Gabriel. *Wealth and Power in America.* New York: Praeger, 1962.

Krutch, Joseph Wood. *Human Nature and the Human Condition.* New York: Random House, 1959.

Leven, Maurice, Harold G. Moulton, and Clark Warburton. *America's Capacity to Consume.* New York: Review of Reviews, 1934.

Morgan, James N., Martin H. David, Wilbur J. Cohen, and Harry E. Brazer. *Income and Welfare in the United States.* New York: McGraw-Hill, 1962.

Nourse, Edwin G., et al. *America's Capacity to Produce.* New York: Review of Reviews, 1934.

Parker, Richard. *The Myth of the Middle Class.* New York: Harper and Row, 1972.

Patterson, James T. *America's Struggle against Poverty, 1900–1980.* Cambridge: Harvard University Press, 1981.

Riesman, David, with Nathan Glazer and Revel Denny. *The Lonely Crowd.* New Haven: Yale University Press, 1950.

Rogers, Harrel. *Poor Women, Poor Families.* Armonk, N.Y.: Sharpe, 1986.

Ryan, William. *Blaming the Victim.* New York: Pantheon, 1971.

Shannon, David A., ed. *The Great Depression.* New York: Prentice-Hall, Spectrum, 1960.

Trattner, Walter I. *A History of Social Welfare in America.* New York: Macmillan, 1974.

Wootton, Barbara. *The Social Foundations of British Wage Policy.* London: Unwin, 1964.

CHAPTER 4: BLACKS, HISPANICS, AMERICAN INDIANS, AND POVERTY— AND WHAT WORKED BY GARY D. SANDEFUR

Notes

This research was supported by grants provided by the Department of Health and Human Services, Assistant Secretary for Planning and Evaluation, to the Institute for Research on Poverty, and by the National Institute for Child Health and Human Development to the Center for Demography and Ecology. The views expressed are those of the author and not those of the funding institutions. I thank Betty Evanson for her editorial advice and suggestions.

1. National Advisory Commission, p. 237.
2. Ibid., p. 260.
3. Wilson, *The Truly Disadvantaged;* Kasarda, "Redistribution."

4. U.S. Bureau of the Census, *Poverty 1985.*

5. Tienda and Jensen, "Poverty and Minorities."

6. The other Hispanics include people of Cuban, Central American, and South American descent. Hispanics may be of any race.

7. Sandefur and Sakamoto, "Household Structure." Part of the improvement for American Indians may have been due to changes in self-identification that occurred between 1969 and 1979 (Passel and Berman, "Quality of 1980 Census Data"). There was little change in self-identification in traditional Indian areas.

8. Smith, "Poverty and the Family."

9. U.S. Bureau of the Census, *Poverty 1985,* Table 4, pp. 21–22.

10. Smolensky et al., "Declining Significance."

11. U.S. Bureau of the Census, *Estimates of Poverty 1983.*

12. U.S. Bureau of the Census, *Census 1980: American Indians, Eskimos, and Aleuts.*

13. Gramlich, "The Main Themes," p. 343.

14. Bassi and Ashenfelter, "Job Creation and Training," p. 149.

15. Gramlich, "The Main Themes."

16. Smith and Welch, *Closing the Gap.*

17. Wilson, *The Truly Disadvantaged,* p. 124.

18. Smith and Welch, *Closing the Gap.*

19. Sorkin, *American Indians.*

20. Glazer, "Education and Training Programs"; Jencks, "Comment on Glazer."

21. Jencks, "Comment on Glazer," p. 179.

22. Sandefur, "Duality in Federal Policy."

23. Bell, "The Remedy in *Brown.*"

24. Hauser, "College Entry" and "Post-High-School Plans." Hauser's conclusion that cutbacks in financial aid may help account for the decline in the proportion of recent black high school graduates who attended college between 1977 and 1983 is based on his finding that other factors, including family income, do not explain the decline.

25. The Kerner Report contained more detailed recommendations for changes in several aspects of the welfare system in place in 1968: standards of assistance, extension of AFDC-UP, financing, work incentives and training, removal of freeze on recipients, restrictions on eligibility, and miscellaneous other features. I have focused on what I consider the key elements of these proposals in my discussion in the text.

26. This is similar to the Wisconsin child-support experiment designed by Irwin Garfinkel and colleagues at the Institute for Research on Poverty.

27. E.g., Danziger, "Antipoverty Policy."

28. Danziger, Haveman, and Plotnick, "Antipoverty Policy: Effects," p. 74.

29. Ellwood and Summers, "Poverty in America," p. 97.

30. Starr, "Health Care for the Poor."

31. Ibid.; Okada and Wan, "Impact of Community Health Services"; Sandefur, "Duality in Federal Policy."

32. It is important to emphasize that I am talking about poverty and not about other features of central-city life such as drug use and crime. These and other central-city problems may require solutions that are directed specifically at central cities.

Sources

Bassi, Laurie J., and Orley Ashenfelter. "The Effect of Direct Job Creation and Training Programs on Low-Skilled Workers." In Danziger and Weinberg.

Bell, Derrick A., Jr. "The Remedy in *Brown* Is Effective Schooling for Black Children." *Social Policy,* Fall 1984, pp. 8–15.

Danziger, Sheldon H. "Antipoverty Policy and Welfare Reform." Paper presented at the Rockefeller Foundation Conference on Welfare Reform, Williamsburg, Va., February 16–18, 1988.

Danziger, Sheldon H., Robert H. Haveman, and Robert D. Plotnick. "Antipoverty Policy: Effects on the Poor and the Nonpoor." In Danziger and Weinberg.

Danziger, Sheldon H., and Daniel H. Weinberg, eds. *Fighting Poverty: What Works and What Doesn't.* Cambridge: Harvard University Press, 1986.

Ellwood, David T., and Lawrence H. Summers. "Poverty in America: Is Welfare the Answer or the Problem?" In Danziger and Weinberg.

Glazer, Nathan. "Education and Training Programs and Poverty." In Danziger and Weinberg.

Gramlich, Edward M. "The Main Themes." In Danziger and Weinberg.

Hauser, Robert M. "College Entry among Black High School Graduates: Family Income Does Not Explain the Decline." Working paper no.

87-19, Center for Demography and Ecology, University of Wisconsin at Madison.

Hauser, Robert M. "Post-High-School Plans of Black High-School Graduates: What Has Changed since the Mid-1970s?" Working paper no. 87-26, Center for Demography and Ecology, University of Wisconsin at Madison.

Jencks, Christopher. "Comment on Glazer." In Danziger and Weinberg.

Kasarda, John D. "The Regional and Urban Redistribution of People and Jobs in the U.S." Paper presented to the Committee on National Urban Policy, National Research Council, Washington, D.C., October 1986.

Leonard, Jonathan S. "The Effectiveness of Equal Employment Law and Affirmative Action Regulation." Working paper no. 1745, National Bureau of Economic Research, Cambridge, Mass., 1985.

———. "The Impact of Affirmative Action on Employment." *Journal of Labor Economics,* vol. 2 (1984), pp. 439–63.

National Advisory Commission on Civil Disorders. *Report* (Kerner Report). New York: Dutton, 1968.

Nickens, Herbert. "Health Problems of Minority Groups: Public Health's Unfinished Agenda." *Public Health Reports,* vol. 101, no. 3 (May–June 1986), pp. 230–31.

Okada, Louise M., and Thomas T. H. Wan. "Impact of Community Health Services and Medicaid on the Use of Health Services." *Public Health Reports,* vol. 95, no. 6 (November–December 1980), pp. 520–34.

Passel, Jeffrey, and Patricia Berman. "Quality of 1980 Census Data for American Indians." Paper presented at the meeting of the American Statistical Association, Las Vegas, Nev., August 1985.

Sandefur, Gary D. "The Duality in Federal Policy toward Minority Groups, 1787–1987." In Sandefur and Tienda.

Sandefur, Gary D., and Arthur Sakamoto. "American Indian Household Structure and Income." *Demography,* vol. 25, no. 1 (February 1988), pp. 71–80.

Sandefur, Gary D., and Marta Tienda, eds. *Minorities, Poverty, and Social Policy.* New York: Plenum, 1988.

Smith, James P. "Poverty and the Family." In Sandefur and Tienda.

Smith, James P., and Finis R. Welch. *Closing the Gap: Forty Years of Economic Progress for Blacks.* Santa Monica: Rand, 1988.

Smolensky, Eugene, Sheldon H. Danziger, and Peter Gottschalk. "The Declining Significance of Age: Trends in the Well-Being of Children and the Elderly since 1939." In T. Smeeding, J. Palmer, and B. Torrey, eds. *The Changing Well-Being of the Aged and Children in the United States.* Washington, D.C.: Urban Institute, 1988.

Sorkin, Alan. *American Indians and Federal Aid.* Washington, D.C.: Brookings Institution, 1972.

Starr, Paul. "Health Care for the Poor: The Past Twenty Years." In Danziger and Weinberg.

Tienda, Marta, and Leif Jensen. "Poverty and Minorities: A Quarter-Century Profile of Color and Socioeconomic Disadvantage." In Sandefur and Tienda.

U.S. Bureau of the Census. *Census of the United States, 1970: Characteristics of the American Indian Population.* Washington, D.C.: Government Printing Office, 1974.

———. *Census of the United States, 1970: Characteristics of the Low-Income Population.* Washington, D.C.: Government Printing Office, 1974.

———. *Census of the United States, 1980: American Indians, Eskimos, and Aleuts on Identified Reservations and in the Historic Areas of Oklahoma (Excluding Urbanized Areas).* Washington, D.C.: Government Printing Office, 1986.

———. *Census of the United States, 1980: General Social and Economic Characteristics.* Washington, D.C.: Government Printing Office, 1983.

———. *Estimates of Poverty Including the Value of Noncash Benefits: 1983.* Washington, D.C.: Government Printing Office, 1984.

———. *Poverty in the United States, 1985.* Washington, D.C.: Government Printing Office, 1987.

Wilson, William Julius. *The Declining Significance of Race.* Chicago: University of Chicago Press, 1978.

———. *The Truly Disadvantaged: The Inner City, the Underclass, and Public Policy.* Chicago: University of Chicago Press, 1987.

Working Seminar on Family and American Welfare Policy. *The New Consensus on Family and Welfare.* Washington, D.C.: American Enterprise Institute for Public Policy Research, 1987.

CHAPTER 5: THE PERSISTENCE OF URBAN POVERTY BY TERRY K. ADAMS, GREG J. DUNCAN, AND WILLARD L. RODGERS

Notes

The research reported in this chapter was supported by a grant from the Rockefeller Foundation. Lee Bawden and Joan Maxwell have assisted us at various stages, but they are not responsible for the methods used or interpretations expressed in this paper. We are grateful to Dorothy Duncan, Ronald Mincy, Richard Nathan, and Dan Weinberg for providing helpful comments, and to Deborah Laren, Dawn Von Thurn, and Lynn Dielman for research assistance.

1. Auletta's series became a book, *The Underclass.*

2. Trends in deviant behavior were prominent in Charles Murray's indictment of Great Society programs in *Losing Ground.*

3. Bane and Jargowsky, in "Urban Poverty," provide a detailed profile of the geographic concentration of urban poverty in 1970 and 1980, and are the first to highlight the three dimensions—behavior, geography, and persistence—of urban poverty discussed here.

4. For instance, Wilson, *The Truly Disadvantaged.*

5. Sewell and Hauser *(Education, Occupation, and Earnings)* find especially strong effects of income on the early career attainments of men. Hill and Duncan ("Parental Family Income") find significant effects of parental income on schooling and wage rates of both men and women. Both of these studies find that income effects persist even after adjustments for differences in parental schooling and occupational attainment.

6. Corcoran et al., "Intergenerational Transmission."

7. Bane and Ellwood, "Slipping Into and Out of Poverty."

8. Auletta's underclass is equal to the number of people whose incomes, not including government transfers, were below the poverty level in at least three of five years.

9. Ricketts and Sawhill, "Defining and Measuring the Underclass."

10. Bane and Jargowsky, "Urban Poverty."

11. Our profile of persistent poverty uses the 1975–84 years of the

panel; our analysis of changes in the persistence of urban poverty uses all years, 1968–84. A number of investigations of the quality of the PSID data suggest that they ought to provide reasonably representative estimates of the population in those years (Becketti et al., *Attrition from the PSID;* Duncan, Hill, and Ponza, *How Representative Is the PSID?*). However, in both long-term studies like the PSID and in Census Bureau surveys, some subsets of the urban poor will be better represented than others—welfare recipients with traceable addresses and kin networks can be followed successfully; homeless individuals without close connections to kin cannot.

Since we matched some of our analyses to 1980 census information, we used an individual's place of residence in 1980 to determine whether he was urban. The U.S. Department of Agriculture's Beale Urbanicity Code of 0 is assigned to the 56 counties (out of 3,137) defined as central counties in metropolitan areas with populations above 1 million; we defined as urban anyone living in any of those 56 counties in 1980, though he may have lived elsewhere in other years. A definition of urbanicity based on city boundaries rather than counties would be preferable in some respects, but our choice was constrained by the available data. Nonetheless, the correlation is fairly high: the largest 13 cities, and 36 of the largest 50, were in Beale Code 0 counties; so are 28 percent of the people in the United States.

12. To make our data comparable to Census Bureau data, we also deflated the incomes of PSID households to give overall poverty counts identical to those of the 1980 census. We defined income, as does the Census Bureau in computing poverty status, to include all *money* income (including cash welfare and social-insurance payments) but not food stamps, medical insurance, and other *in-kind* income. Aggregate income estimates based on reports of census respondents are often less than those obtained from institutional sources such as employer payrolls and government income-maintenance programs. Aggregate income estimates based on the Current Population Survey and the Decennial Census, for example, typically produce only 75 to 80 percent of the AFDC and General Assistance income reported by state and federal welfare agencies. Estimates from the PSID and the Census Bureau's Survey of Income and Program Participation, on the other hand, are substantially higher proportions of the institutional totals. In order to ensure that our poverty rates conformed to those of the decennial census, it was necessary for us to adjust incomes reported in the PSID so they are underreported to the same extent as they apparently are in the Decennial Census data. Using information from the

County-City Databook, we calculated that persons living in the Beale Code 0 counties in 1980 had a poverty rate (weighted for population) of 13.4 percent. We then found the adjustment to the income of the PSID Beale Code 0 county residents that produced a PSID (weighted) poverty rate of 13.4 percent. That adjustment turned out to be division by a factor of 1.42. The total household money incomes in our PSID subset, therefore, are the reported incomes divided by 1.42.

13. Computation from county-city data file for 56 urban (Beale Code 0) counties, weighted by total population. The average annual poverty rate for 1974–83 was about 13 percent (*Statistical Abstract of the United States, 1986,* Table 766).

14. For other ethnic groups, such as Hispanics, samples were too small to permit precise analysis. They are therefore grouped with whites here and throughout this chapter.

15. "Substantial work" was defined as at least 1000 hours in 1979 by the head of the household and the head's spouse, if present. That would be the equivalent of a half-time job (20 hours a week) for the full year, or 40 hours a week for half a year.

16. The PSID data currently available are based on ZIP Code areas, which usually have four or five times the population of the smaller census tracts; thus it is hard to isolate fairly small pockets of high poverty. Here we identified the ZIP Code area of the 1979 residence of each sample individual, and then matched them to the census-based data on what fraction of the population in each area was poor in 1979. Following the research of others, we classified the samples according to whether 20, 30, or 40 percent of the people in their area were poor. Since other researchers had found variations based on ethnicity, we also divided the PSID sample by ethnicity, although small sample sizes, especially for persistently poor whites, render some of our estimates rather imprecise.

17. The PSID figures show only 8 percent of poor blacks living in ZIP Code areas with poverty rates of 40 percent and above; the Census Bureau figures show 36 percent of poor blacks living in census tracts (smaller areas, it must be remembered) with rates of 40 percent or above. This suggests that poor blacks living in small and somewhat isolated areas of concentrated poverty do not show up in the ZIP Code-based figures, since a ZIP area could contain a 40-percent census tract along with more prosperous tracts, and thus average, say, 15 or 20 percent. A ZIP area may be larger than a square mile; those with a high concentration of poverty almost always

contain several high-poverty census tracts. The fact that the larger ZIP areas have substantially lower concentrations of poor people than the smaller census tracts should make us cautious about designating either area as equivalent to a social neighborhood and about analyzing migration between areas. A move across the street may take a family from one census tract to another, while a move to a house several census tracts away could still be within the same ZIP area.

18. Counts of total city populations and of one-year poor populations in 1979 come from the city-level columns in the 1980 Census Bureau publications series PH-C-80-2 (Census Tracts) for the relevant Metropolitan Statistical Areas, Tables P-11 and P-15. The figures for the one-year poor, broken down into several categories of age and ethnicity, are multiplied by our estimates (based on the PSID data and detailed in Adams and Duncan, "The Persistence of Urban Poverty") of the fraction of poor individuals within those categories who are persistently poor.

19. We can illustrate our procedures with the case of transitions out of poverty. Using a cutoff of 125 percent of the official poverty line as our working definition, we first estimated the probability of a transition out of poverty between calendar years 1969 and 1970. For the base population—those eligible to make the transition—we selected individuals living in Beale Code 0 counties in both years and in households with incomes (as reported by respondents, and *not* adjusted to match Census Bureau poverty rates as in the analyses reported above) below the 125 percent cutoff in 1969; whether they had made the transition out of poverty was based on the income of the households in which they lived in 1970. Analogous procedures produced a somewhat different sample for each of the succeeding pairs of years, ending with 1982–83, the most recent year of available data. Similar procedures applied to individuals living outside Beale Code 0 counties produced comparison samples to show whether the trends observed in urban areas prevailed elsewhere as well. The probability of exit from poverty varies as the composition of the poor population changes; therefore we pay special attention to the trends in the characteristics of the population.

20. We did this through a logistic multiple regression analysis of the escape probabilities, in which calendar year, demographic characteristics, and family income one year and two years prior to the possible transition out of poverty were added sequentially to the regressions. If, for example, unfavorable demographic changes have made it more difficult for the urban

poor to escape, then we would expect regression controls for the demographic factors to reduce the differences between high escape probabilities at the beginning of the period and low probabilities at the end.

21. We performed a parallel analysis of the transitions ("entries") into poverty among the urban nonpoor and found less evidence of change from the late 1960s to the early 1980s. Rates of entry into poverty by persons not poor in the previous year were relatively high (between 4 and 5 percent) in the late 1960s and early 1970s, fell substantially in the mid-1970s, and have risen slowly since then, resulting in little net change between the beginning and end of the period. Demographic changes over the period favored staying out of poverty; had they not occurred, the chances that a nonpoor individual living in a highly urbanized county would fall into poverty would have been much higher at the end of the period than at the beginning.

Sources

Adams, Terry K., and Greg J. Duncan. "The Persistence of Urban Poverty and Its Demographic and Behavioral Correlates." Mimeo. Survey Research Center, 1988.

Auletta, Kenneth. *The Underclass.* New York: Random House, 1982.

Bane, Mary J., and D. Ellwood. "Slipping Into and Out of Poverty: The Dynamics of Spells." *Journal of Human Resources,* vol. 21 (1986), pp. 1–23.

Bane, Mary J., and Paul A. Jargowsky. "Urban Poverty and the Underclass: Basic Questions." Paper presented at the APPAM Conference, Washington, D.C., October 1987.

Becketti, S., W. Gould, L. Lillard, and F. Welch. *Attrition from the PSID.* Los Angeles: Unicon Research Corp., 1983.

Corcoran, Mary, Roger H. Gordon, Deborah Laren, and Gary Solon. "Intergenerational Transmission of Education, Income, and Earnings." Mimeograph. Ann Arbor: University of Michigan, 1987.

Danziger, Sheldon, and Peter Gottschalk. "Earnings Inequality, the Spatial Concentration of Poverty, and the Underclass." *American Economic Review,* vol. 77, no. 2 (May 1987), pp. 211–15.

Duncan, Greg J., Martha S. Hill, and Michael Ponza. *How Representative Is the PSID? A Response to Some Questions Raised in the Unicon Report.* Ann Arbor: Institute for Social Research, 1984.

Duncan, Greg J., and Willard L. Rodgers. "A Demographic Analysis of Childhood Poverty." Working paper. Ann Arbor: Survey Research Center, University of Michigan, 1985.

Hill, Martha S., and Greg J. Duncan. "Parental Family Income and the Socioeconomic Attainment of Children." *Social Science Research,* vol. 16 (1987), pp. 39–73.

Murray, Charles. *Losing Ground.* New York: Basic Books, 1984.

Ricketts, Erol R., and Isabel Sawhill, "Defining and Measuring the Underclass." Paper presented at the meeting of the American Economics Association, December 1986.

Sewall, W. H., and R. M. Hauser. *Education, Occupation, and Earnings: Achievement in the Early Career.* New York: Academic Press, 1975.

Survey Research Center. *User Guide to the Panel Study of Income Dynamics.* Ann Arbor: University of Michigan, 1984.

Wilson, William Julius. "Cycles of Deprivation and the Underclass Debate." *Social Service Review,* vol. 59 (December 1985), pp. 541–59.

———. "Social Policy and Minority Groups." Institute for Research on Poverty Conference Paper. University of Wisconsin at Madison, 1986.

———. *The Truly Disadvantaged.* Chicago: University of Chicago Press, 1987.

CHAPTER 6: SEPARATE SOCIETIES: HAVE THE KERNER WARNINGS COME TRUE? BY GARY ORFIELD

Notes

1. Johnson, *The Vantage Point,* pp. 172–73.

2. Dent, *The Prodigal South*, pp. 73–156.

3. Murray, *Losing Ground;* Kemp, *An American Renaissance,* chapter 3; Stockman, *The Triumph of Politics,* pp. 19–108.

4. This chapter does not deal with the situation of urban Hispanics. A new Kerner Commission would investigate the extremely threatening trends in Hispanic education, economic displacement, and inequality in central-city barrios and recommend action to prevent three-way fragmentation of society in the largest cities.

5. McKinney and Schnare, *Trends in Residential Segregation,* tables 2, 3, and 4.

6. Ibid., p. 16.

7. Ibid., table 2.

8. Farley and Wilger, *Recent Changes,* pp. 1–6; Wilger, "Black-White Residential Segregation," pp. 7–11; Jakubs, "Recent Racial Segregation."

9. Ibid., p. 158.

10. Kain, "Black Suburbanization," pp. 253–84.

11. Farley and Wilger, *Recent Changes,* p. 11.

12. Yinger, "Racial Dimension"; Feins and Bratt, "Barred in Boston"; Peterman and Hunt, "Fair Housing Audit Inventory"; Schlay, "Credit on Color"; Listokin and Casey, *Mortgage Lending and Race.*

13. Taub, Taylor, and Dunham, *Paths of Neighborhood Change.*

14. Senate Subcommittee on Housing and Urban Affairs, 1987.

15. Shlay, "Credit on Color."

16. Orfield, Woolbright, and Kim, "Neighborhood Change."

17. Slessarev, "Economic Growth, Job Training, and Racial Inequality in Metropolitan Atlanta."

18. Kasarda, "People and Jobs on the Move."

19. Fossett, "The Downside of Housing Booms"; Fossett and Orfield, "Market Failure and Federal Policy."

20. Orfield, *Public School Desegregation,* appendix B.

21. 418 U.S. 717; Dimond, *Beyond Busing.*

22. Orfield and Monfort, "Are American Schools Resegregating?"

23. Orfield, Mitzel, et al., *The Chicago Study.*

24. Garrett, "Metropolitan Chicago Public High Schools"; Jaeger, "Minority and Low Income High Schools"; Peskin, "Metropolitan Atlanta High Schools"; Witte, "Race and Educational Inequalities in Milwaukee."

25. Orfield and Monfort, *Racial Change and Desegregation.*

26. Harris Survey, American Council on Education Survey of College Freshmen; data reported in *Focus,* July 1987, p. 6.

Sources

Crain, Robert L. "The Long-Term Effects of Desegregation: Results from a True Experiment." Paper prepared for National Conference on School Desegregation Research, Chicago, September 1986.

Crain, Robert L., and Carol Sachs Weisman. *Discrimination, Personality, and Achievement: A Survey of Northern Blacks.* New York: Seminar Press, 1972.

Darden, Joe T., Richard Child Hill, June Thomas, and Richard Thomas. *Detroit: Race and Uneven Development.* Philadelphia: Temple University Press, 1987.

Dent, Harry S. *The Prodigal South Returns to Power.* New York: John Wiley, 1978.

Dimond, Paul R. *Beyond Busing: Inside the Challenge to Urban Segregation.* Ann Arbor: University of Michigan Press, 1985.

Farley, Reynolds, and Robert Wilger. *Recent Changes in Residential Segregation of Blacks from Whites: An Analysis of 203 Metropolises.* Report no. 15, National Academy of Sciences, May 1987.

Feins, Judy D., and Rachel C. Bratt. "Barred in Boston: Racial Discrimination in Housing." *Journal of the American Planning Association,* vol. 49 (1983), pp. 344–55.

Feliciano, Zadia. "Dropouts, Poverty, and the New California School Reforms." Working paper no. 9, Metropolitan Opportunity Project, University of Chicago, February 1988.

Fossett, James W. "The Downside of Housing Booms: Low Income Housing in Atlanta, 1970–1986." Working paper, Metropolitan Opportunity Project, University of Chicago, September 1987.

Fossett, James W., and Gary Orfield. "Market Failure and Federal Policy: Low Income Housing in Chicago, 1970–1983." In Tobin, *Divided Neighborhoods,* pp. 158–80.

Garrett, Jim. "Metropolitan Chicago Public High Schools: Race, Poverty, and Educational Opportunity." Working paper no. 5, Metropolitan Opportunity Project, University of Chicago, June 1987.

Jaeger, Christopher. "Minority and Low Income High Schools: Evidence of Educational Inequality in Metro Los Angeles." Working paper no. 8, Metropolitan Opportunity Project, University of Chicago, October 1987.

Jakubs, John F. "Recent Racial Segregation in U.S. SMSAs." *Urban Geography,* vol. 7, no. 2 (1986), pp. 146–63.

Johnson, Lyndon B. *The Vantage Point: Perspectives of the Presidency, 1963–1969.* New York: Holt, 1971.

Kain, John F. "Black Suburbanization in the Eighties: A New Beginning or a False Hope?" In John M. Quigley and Daniel L. Rubin, eds.,

American Domestic Priorities: An Economic Appraisal. Berkeley: University of California Press, 1985.

Kasarda, John. "People and Jobs on the Move: America's New Spatial Dynamics." Paper presented at conference on America's New Economic Geography, Washington, D.C., April 1987.

Kemp, Jack. *An American Renaissance: A Strategy for the 1980s.* New York: Harper and Row, 1979.

Listokin, David, and Stephen Casey. *Mortgage Lending and Race: Conceptual and Analytical Perspectives on the Urban Financing Problem.* New Brunswick: Rutgers Center for Urban Policy Research, 1980.

Massey, Douglas S., and Nancy A. Denton. "Trends in the Residential Segregation of Blacks, Hispanics, and Asians: 1970–1980." *American Sociological Review,* vol. 52 (December 1987), pp. 802–25.

McKinney, Scott, and Ann B. Schnare. *Trends in Residential Segregation by Race.* Project report no. 3672. Washington, D.C.: Urban Institute, 1986.

Murray, Charles. *Losing Ground: American Social Policy, 1950–1980.* New York: Basic Books, 1984.

Newburger, Harriet. "Recent Evidence on Discrimination in Housing." Unpublished report to U.S. Dept. of Housing and Urban Development, 1984.

Orfield, Gary. "The Growth and Concentration of Hispanic Enrollment and the Future of American Education." Paper prepared for National Council of La Raza, Washington, D.C., July 1988.

———. *Public School Desegregation in the United States, 1968–1980.* Washington, D.C.: Joint Center for Political Studies, 1983.

Orfield, Gary, ed. *Fair Housing in Metropolitan Chicago: Perspectives after Two Decades.* Chicago: Chicago Area Fair Housing Alliance, 1987.

Orfield, Gary, Rosemary George, and Amy Orfield. "Racial Change in American Public Schools, 1968–84." Working paper no. 1, National School Desegregation Project, September 1986.

Orfield, Gary, Howard Mitzel, et al. *The Chicago Study of Access and Choice in Higher Education.* Report to the Illinois Senate Committee on Higher Education, 1984.

Orfield, Gary, and Franklin Monfort. "Are American Schools Resegregating in the Reagan Era? A Statistical Analysis of Segregation Levels from 1980 to 1984." Paper presented at National School Desegregation Policy Conference, Brookings Institution, Washington, D.C. November 1986.

———. *Racial Change and Desegregation in Large School Districts: Trends through the 1986–1987 School Year*. Alexandria, Va.: National Association of School Boards, 1988.

Orfield, Gary, Franklin Monfort, and Rosemary George. "School Segregation in the 1980s: Trends in the States and Metropolitan Areas." Washington, D.C.: Joint Center for Political Studies, July 1987.

Orfield, Gary, Albert Woolbright, and Helene Kim. "Neighborhood Change and Integration in Metropolitan Chicago." Chicago: Leadership Council for Metropolitan Open Communities, 1984.

Pearce, Diana. "Breaking Down Barriers: New Evidence on the Impact of Metropolitan Desegregation on Housing Patterns." Report to the National Institute of Education, 1980.

Peskin, Lawrence. "Metropolitan Atlanta High Schools." Working paper, Metropolitan Opportunity Project, University of Chicago, 1988.

Peterman, William, and Kim Hunt. "Fair Housing Audit Inventory for Metropolitan Chicago." In Orfield, *Fair Housing*, pp. 445–97.

Rosenbaum, James E. "School Experiences of Low-Income Black Children in White Suburbs." Paper prepared for National Conference on School Desegregation Research, September 1986.

Schnare, Ann B. "Residential Segregation by Race in U.S. Metropolitan Areas: An Analysis across Cities and over Time." Washington, D.C.: Urban Institute, Contract no. 246-2, February 1977.

Shlay, Anne B. "Credit on Color: Segregation, Racial Transition, and Housing-Credit Flows." In Orfield, *Fair Housing*, pp. 109–88.

Slessarev, Helene. "Economic Growth, Job Training, and Racial Inequality in Metropolitan Atlanta." Working paper, Metropolitan Opportunity Project, University of Chicago, 1987.

Stockman, David A. *The Triumph of Politics: The Inside Story of the Reagan Revolution.* New York: Avon Books, 1987.

Taeuber, Karl. "Racial Residential Segregation, 1980." In Citizens' Commission on Civil Rights, *A Decent Home.* Washington, D.C.: 1983, appendix.

Taub, Richard P., D. Garth Taylor, and Jan P. Dunham. *Paths of Neighborhood Change.* Chicago: University of Chicago Press, 1984.

Tobin, Gary, ed. *Divided Neighborhoods: Changing Patterns of Racial Segregation.* Beverly Hills: Sage, 1987.

U.S. Bureau of the Census. *Geographical Mobility: 1985.* Current Population Reports, series P-20, no. 420. Washington, D.C.: Government Printing Office, 1987.

U.S. National Advisory Commission on Civil Disorders. *Report* (Kerner Report). New York: Bantam Books, 1968.

U.S. National Advisory Commission on Civil Disorders. *Supplemental Studies.* New York: Praeger, 1968.

Walsh, Daniel J. "SES, Academic Achievement, and Reorganization of Metropolitan Area Schools: Preliminary Implications of the Milwaukee Area Study." *Metropolitan Education,* no. 1 (Spring 1986), pp. 92–99.

Wilger, Robert J. "Black-White Residential Segregation in 1980: Have Civil-Rights Laws Made a Difference?" University of Michigan Population Studies Center, October 1987.

Witte, John. "Race and Educational Inequalities in Milwaukee: Evidence and Implications." Paper prepared for National Conference on School Desegregation Research, 1986.

Yinger, John. "The Racial Dimension of Urban Housing Markets in the 1980s." In Tobin, *Divided Neighborhoods*, pp. 43–67.

CHAPTER 7: THE GHETTO UNDERCLASS AND THE CHANGING STRUCTURE OF URBAN POVERTY BY WILLIAM JULIUS WILSON, ROBERT APONTE, JOLEEN KIRSCHENMAN, AND LOÏC J. D. WACQUANT

Notes

The authors gratefully acknowledge the financial support of the Ford Foundation, the Carnegie Corporation, the U.S. Department of Health and Human Services, the Institute for Research on Poverty, the Joyce Foundation, the Lloyd A. Fry Foundation, the Rockefeller Foundation, the William T. Grant Foundation, the Woods Charitable Fund, and the Chicago Community Trust.

1. Meranto, *The Kerner Report Revisited.*
2. Shapiro, "The Ghetto."

3. Reischauer, "Geographic Concentration."

4. There are important regional variations in the evolution of these ten cities, but space limitations permit us only to trace aggregate trends here. For a city-by-city analysis that highlights the contrasts between Rust Belt and Sun Belt metropolises, especially as regards joblessness and deindustrialization, see Wacquant and Wilson, "Poverty, Joblessness, and Social Transformation."

5. A "community area" is a statistical unit conceived by the Chicago school of urban sociology in the 1930s. It consists of a number of adjacent census tracts, generally containing neighborhoods of similar racial and ecological makeup. A "poverty community area" is defined here as a community area with at least 20 percent of its families below the official poverty line.

6. The number near each dot on the figure identifies the community area by poverty ranking in 1980 as given in Table 7.3.

7. For an elaboration, see Wilson, *The Truly Disadvantaged.*

8. Drake and Cayton, *Black Metropolis.*

9. Kasarda, "Urbanization, Community, and the Metropolitan Problems."

10. Kasarda, "Caught in the Web."

11. "White-collar service industries" are "defined as those service industries where executives, managers, professionals, and clerical employees exceed more than 50% of the industry workforce" (Kasarda, "Regional and Urban Redistribution," pp. 18–19).

12. Levy, "Poverty and Economic Growth," p. 9.

13. Ibid., pp. 19–20.

14. Ibid., p. 19.

15. Lichter, "Racial Differences," p. 789.

16. For a more detailed discussion of the following arguments, see Wilson, *The Truly Disadvantaged.*

17. Murray, *Losing Ground;* Mead, *Beyond Entitlement.*

18. See, for instance, Wilson, *The Truly Disadvantaged,* and Sosin, "Review of *Beyond Entitlement.*"

19. Danziger and Gottschalk, "Poverty of Losing Ground."

Sources

Chicago Fact Book Consortium. *Local Community Fact Book: Chicago Metropolitan Area.* Chicago: Chicago Review Press, 1984.

Danziger, Sheldon, and Peter Gottschalk. "The Poverty of Losing Ground." *Challenge,* May–June 1985.

Drake, St. Clair, and Horace R. Cayton. *Black Metropolis: A Study of Negro Life in a Northern City.* New York: Harper and Row, 1962 (first published in 1945).

Kasarda, J. D. "Caught in the Web of Change." *Society,* vol. 21 (1983), pp. 4–7.

———. "The Regional and Urban Redistribution of People and Jobs in the U.S." Paper prepared for the National Research Council Committee on National Urban Policy, National Academy of Sciences, Washington, D.C., 1986.

———. "Urbanization, Community, and the Metropolitan Problems." In *Handbook of Contemporary Urban Life: An Examination of Urbanization, Social Organization, and Metropolitan Politics,* ed. David Street et al. San Francisco: Jossey-Bass, 1978.

Levy, F. "Poverty and Economic Growth." Unpublished draft. University of Maryland, College Park, 1986.

Lichter, Daniel T. "Racial Differences in Underemployment in American Cities." *American Journal of Sociology,* vol. 93, no. 4 (1988), pp. 771–92.

Mead, Lawrence M. *Beyond Entitlement: The Social Obligations of Citizenship.* New York: Free Press, 1986.

Meranto, Philip. "The Kerner Report Revisited: An Overview." In *The Kerner Report Revisited,* ed. Philip Meranto. University of Illinois Bulletin, vol. 67, no. 121 (1970), pp. 9–12.

Murray, Charles. *Losing Ground: American Social Policy, 1950–1980.* New York: Basic Books, 1984.

Reischauer, R. "The Geographic Concentration of Poverty: What Do We Know?" Unpublished draft. Brookings Institution, Washington, D.C., March 1987.

Shapiro, Walter. "The Ghetto: From Bad to Worse." *Time,* August 24, 1987, pp. 18–19.

Sosin, M. "Review of *Beyond Entitlement.*" *Social Service Review,* vol. 61 (March 1987), pp. 156–59.

U.S. Bureau of the Census. *Census of Population: 1970,* Subject Reports, "Low Income Areas in Large Cities." PC(2)-9B. Washington, D.C.: Government Printing Office, 1973.

———. *Census of Population: 1980,* Subject Reports, "Poverty Areas in

Large Cities." PC-80-2-8D. Washington, D.C.: Government Printing Office, 1985.

———. "Characteristics of the Population Below the Poverty Level: 1978." In *Current Population Reports.* Series P-60, no. 124 (1980).

Wacquant, Loïc J. D., and William Julius Wilson. "Poverty, Joblessness, and the Social Transformation of the Inner City." Forthcoming in David Ellwood and Phoebe Cottingham (eds.), *Reforming Welfare Policy: What Works and What Doesn't*. Cambridge, Mass.: Harvard University Press, 1989.

Wilson, William Julius. *The Truly Disadvantaged: The Inner City, the Underclass, and Public Policy.* Chicago: University of Chicago Press, 1987.

CHAPTER 8: THOMAS JEFFERSON, THE KERNER COMMISSION, AND THE RETREAT OF FOLLY BY LYNN A. CURTIS

Notes

1. The narrowest definition includes only long-term welfare recipients living in poverty areas, and results in an estimate of an underclass of less than 1 million. The broadest includes people poor in five years out of seven, and results in an estimate of over 10 million.

2. In terms of evaluated outcomes, these programs have many objectives. To illustrate their success, consider just one of the outcomes: the reduction of crime.

Studies by the Vera Institute and the New York Criminal Justice Coordinating Council showed lower recidivism rates for Argus graduates than for graduates from almost any other program in New York City that works with such high-risk offenders. A Philadelphia Psychiatric Center study reported a 3 percent rearrest rate for Umojans compared to a rate of 70 to 90 percent for young people released from conventional juvenile correction facilities. Over a fifteen-year period the number of adjudicated delinquents in the La Playa neighborhood where Centro is located was reduced by 85 percent and the delinquency rate was cut in half, despite a rapid increase in the population of high-risk youth.

In terms of recidivism, Argus, Centro, and Umoja are much more effective than prison. They are also much less expensive than prison. The annual cost per person is $30,087 for New York State prisons, $24,186 for Minnesota prisons, $22,433 for a federal maximum-security prison, and $19,339 for California prisons; while it is only $16,000 for both Argus and Umoja residents, $2,000 for Argus nonresidents, and $200 for Centro nonresidents. (Curtis, "Neighborhood, Family," p. 13.)

3. Kuttner, "Go Left, Democrats."
4. Sandel, "Democrats and Community," p. 23.

Sources

Alperovitz, Gar, and Jeff Faux. *Rebuilding America.* New York: Pantheon, 1984.

Ball-Rokeach, Sandra, and James F. Short, Jr. "Collective Violence." In Curtis, *American Violence.*

Brinkley, J. "Fighting Narcotics Is Everyone's Issue Now." *New York Times,* August 10, 1986, p. E-10.

Broder, David S. "The Dangers of Being Militarily Top-Heavy." *Washington Post,* January 17, 1988, p. C-7.

Brown, Darryl. "Promising, Promising." *Youth Policy,* July 1986, pp. 18–19.

Comer, James P. "Black Violence and Public Policy." In Curtis, *American Violence,* pp. 63–86.

Committee for Economic Development. *Children in Need: Investment Strategies for the Educationally Disadvantaged.* New York, 1987.

Currie, Elliott. *Confronting Crime.* New York: Pantheon, 1985.

Curtis, Lynn A. "Inflation, Economic Policy, and the Inner City." *Annals,* vol. 456 (July 1981), pp. 46–58.

Curtis, Lynn A., ed. *American Violence and Public Policy.* New Haven: Yale University Press, 1985.

Curtis, Lynn A., ed. "Neighborhood, Family, and Employment Strategies." *Annals,* vol. 494 (November 1987).

Edelman, Marian Wright. *Families in Peril: An Agenda for Social Change.* Cambridge: Harvard University Press, 1987.

Etzioni, Amitai. "Socio-Economics: Humanizing the Dismal Science." *Washington Post,* January 11, 1987, p. 83.

Farley, Reynolds, and Walter Allen. *The Color Line and the Quality of Life in America.* New York: Russell Sage, 1987.

Freedman, Samuel G. "Violence Against Blacks Spotlights Racial Strife." *New York Times,* January 2, 1987, p. B-2.

Gibson, Ernest R. "The Poor—Black and White." *Washington Post,* February 24, 1987, p. A-28.

Glasgow, Douglas. "The Black Underclass in Perspective." In *The State of Black America, 1987,* pp. 129–44.

Grant Foundation. "The Forgotten Half: Non-College Youth in America." Interim report, January 1988.

Harris, Irving B. "What Can We Do to Prevent the Cycle of Poverty?" The 1987 Clifford Beers Lecture, Child Study Center, Yale University.

Henderson, Lenneal. "Blacks, Budgets, and Taxes." In *The State of Black America, 1987,* pp. 75–96.

Higginbotham, A. Leon, Jr. *In the Matter of Color.* New York: Oxford University Press, 1978.

Jefferson, Thomas. *Notes on the State of Virginia.* New York: Harpers, 1964 edition.

Kennedy, Paul. *The Rise and Fall of the Great Powers.* New York: Random House, 1987.

Kuttner, Robert. "Go Left, Democrats—Back to Your Roots." *Washington Post,* November 8, 1987, p. C-4.

Ladner, Joyce. *Tomorrow's Tomorrow: The Black Woman.* Garden City, N.J.: Doubleday, 1971.

Lehmann, Nicholas. "The Origins of the Underclass." *Atlantic Monthly,* June 1986, pp. 31–55; July 1986, pp. 54–68.

Liebow, Elliott. *Talley's Corner.* Boston: Little, Brown, 1967.

Manchester, William. *One Brief Shining Moment.* Boston: Little, Brown, 1983.

Murray, Charles. *Losing Ground.* New York: Basic Books, 1984.

National Advisory Commission on Civil Disorders (Kerner Commission). *Report.* Washington, D.C.: U.S. Government Printing Office, 1968.

National Commission on the Causes and Prevention of Violence. *Final Report.* Washington, D.C.: U.S. Government Printing Office, 1969.

Neustadt, Richard E., and Carol F. Steinbach. *Corrective Capitalism: The Rise of America's Community Development Corporations.* New York: Ford Foundation, 1987.

Rainwater, Lee. *Behind Ghetto Walls.* Chicago: Aldine, 1970.

Rowan, Carl. "Tackling the Notion That Some Kids Can't Be Educated." *Washington Post,* January 12, 1988, p. A-21.

Sandel, Michael J. "Democrats and Community." *The New Republic,* February 22, 1988, pp. 20–23.

Schlesinger, Arthur M., Jr. *The Cycles of American History.* Boston: Houghton Mifflin, 1986.

Shanker, Albert. "Eugene Lang's New Path." *New York Times,* February 22, 1987, p. E-9.

Silberman, Charles E. *Criminal Violence, Criminal Justice.* New York: Random House, 1978.

Sturz, Elizabeth. *Widening Circles.* New York: Harper and Row, 1983.

Taggert, Robert. *A Fisherman's Guide.* Kalamazoo: Upjohn Institute, 1981.

Thompson, John W., et al. *Employment and Crime.* Washington, D.C.: U.S. Department of Justice, 1981.

Thurow, Lester. *Dangerous Currents.* New York: Random House, 1983.

Tuchman, Barbara. *The March of Folly.* New York: Ballantine, 1984.

Williams, Juan. "Have We Forgotten the Dream?" *Washington Post,* February 22, 1987, p. C-1.

Wilson, William Julius. *The Truly Disadvantaged.* Chicago: University of Chicago Press, 1987.

THE CONTRIBUTORS

Terry K. Adams, prior to assuming his present position as senior research associate at the Institute for Social Research, University of Michigan, was a legal services attorney. He was associate director of a major study published in David L. Chambers's *Making Fathers Pay*.

Robert Aponte is a doctoral candidate in the Department of Sociology at the University of Chicago and is project coordinator of the Urban Poverty and Family Structure Project there. He is author or coauthor of a number of papers on urban poverty, including "Urban Poverty" in the 1985 *Annual Review of Sociology*.

Lynn A. Curtis is president of the Milton S. Eisenhower Foundation, the private-sector continuation of President Lyndon B. Johnson's 1968 National Commission on the Causes and Prevention of Violence. During the late 1970s, he served as urban-policy advisor to the U. S. Secretary of Housing and Urban Development and as director of President Carter's Urban and Regional Policy Group, later administering a government interagency group on public housing. He is the author or editor of five books and numerous articles.

Greg J. Duncan is program director at the Survey Research Center of the University of Michigan, where he is also codirector of the Panel Study of Income Dynamics project, a twenty-year interview study of the economic and demographic status of American families. He is the author of *Years of Poverty, Years of Plenty,* as well as of numerous articles on poverty and welfare.

David Hamilton is professor emeritus at the University of New Mexico, where he has particularly specialized in social economics and consumer problems. His written work includes *A Primer on the Economics of Poverty* and *The Consumer in Our Economy.*

Fred R. Harris, prior to becoming a professor of political science at the University of New Mexico in 1976, was a member of the U.S. Senate (D., Okla., 1964–73) and a member of the Kerner Commission. He is the author or editor of ten books (two coauthored and one coedited), including *The New Populism* and *America's Democracy: The Ideal and the Reality.*

John Herbers, before he retired in 1987 to teach and write, was a reporter and editor for the *New York Times.* He covered the civil-rights movement in the South in the 1950s and 1960s, and later, as Washington correspondent, reported on Congress, civil rights, and urban affairs. He is the author of four books. He was Ferris Professor of Journalism at Princeton University in 1987–88 and is presently a distinguished lecturer at the University of Maryland.

Joleen Kirschenman is a graduate student in the Department of Sociology at the University of Chicago and is a research assistant for the Urban Poverty and Family Structure Project there. She does research on the industrial restructuring, class transformation, and state politics of advanced industrialized societies.

Gary Orfield is professor of political science at the University of Chicago and the author of numerous works, including *The Reconstruction of Southern Education: The Schools and the 1964 Civil Rights Act* and *Toward a Strategy for Urban Integration: Must We Bus?* A noted consultant and expert witness on civil-rights issues, he currently directs the Metropolitan Opportunity Project, a study of the five largest U.S. metropolitan areas.

Willard L. Rodgers is a senior study director at the Survey Research Center, University of Michigan. In addition to authoring numerous articles on the changing pattern of American marriages and divorce and the economic well-being of children and the elderly, he is the coauthor of *The Quality of American Life.*

Gary D. Sandefur is a professor of social work and sociology at the University of Wisconsin at Madison, where he is also associate director of the Institute for Research on Poverty. He was coeditor of *Minorities, Poverty, and Social Policy* and is the author of numerous articles on racial and ethnic inequality and related subjects.

Roger W. Wilkins was assistant U.S. attorney general during the Johnson administration and later served on the editorial programming staff of the *Washington Post* and as a columnist and member of the editorial board of the *New York Times.* He is presently a senior fellow with the Institute for Policy Studies, Washington, D.C., and Clarence Robinson Professor of History at George Mason University. He is the author of *A Man's Life.*

Loïc J. D. Wacquant is a doctoral student in sociology at the University of Chicago and at the École des Hautes Études en Sciences Sociales in Paris. He has written on colonialism, cultural inequality, and social theory, and his present research interests include class analysis and race and poverty in urban America.

William Julius Wilson, a MacArthur Prize Fellow, is the Lucy Flower Distinguished Service Professor of Sociology and Public Policy at the University of Chicago, where he also directs the Urban Poverty and Family Structure Project. His books include *The Truly Disadvantaged: The Inner City, the Underclass, and Public Policy* and *The Declining Significance of Race.*

INDEX

Italicized page numbers refer to tables and figures.